Inspiring | Educating | Creating | Entertaining

Brimming with creative inspiration, how-to projects, and useful information to enrich your everyday life, Quarto Knows is a favorite destination for those pursuing their interests and passions. Visit our site and dig deeper with our books into your area of interest: Quarto Creates, Quarto Cooks, Quarto Homes, Quarto Lives, Quarto Drives, Quarto Explores, Quarto Gifts, or Quarto Kids.

First published in 2018 by Cool Springs Press, an imprint of The Quarto Group,
401 Second Avenue North, Suite 310, Minneapolis, MN 55401 USA.
T (612) 344-8100 F (612) 344-8692 www.QuartoKnows.com

Cool Springs Press titles are also available at discount for retail, wholesale, promotional, and bulk purchase. For details, contact the Special Sales Manager by email at specialsales@quarto.com or by mail at The Quarto Group, Attn: Special Sales Manager, 401 Second Avenue North, Suite 310, Minneapolis, MN 55401 USA.

10 9 8 7 6 5 4 3 2 1

ISBN: 978-0-7603-6192-4

Digital edition published in 2018
eISBN: 978-0-7603-6193-1

Acquiring Editor: Mark Johanson
Project Managers: Alyssa Bluhm and Nyle Vialet
Art Director: Cindy Samargia Laun
Layout: Silverglass Design

rare varieties • unusual options • plant lore & guidance

MASTERING
the ART of
VEGETABLE
GARDENING

matt mattus

COOL
SPRINGS
PRESS

INTRODUCTION

I guess it was inevitable that I would write a book about vegetable gardening. As some of you who know me know, I am a bona fide plant geek who loves all things horticultural. So, why only vegetables? The answer is simple. I really like to cook, and I really like to eat good food. What better way to ensure you are getting the food you want, raised the way you like it, than to grow it yourself? I look at vegetable gardening not just as a pastime or even a noble expression, but as an essential component of my life. It's not about necessity, as it was in the Depression era. It's not about supporting a patriotic cause, as it was during the World War II years. Honestly, it's not even about saving money, like it was in the 1970s. Today, vegetable gardening is all about quality.

What I mean by quality is having the ability to choose the exact varieties we want to grow and eat, and, even more importantly, having the resources, knowledge, and patience to grow them well. For me, food quality isn't a question of organic versus conventional, or no-till versus digging in, or heirloom versus hybrid. It's a question of what I want to grow, and what I should do to help each seed or plant become the best vegetable it can possibly be.

For over fifty years now, since I was five years old, I have been growing vegetable gardens and searching for the answers to these questions. *Mastering the Art of Vegetable Gardening* is my attempt to share what I have learned in that search so far. Every vegetable discussed in this book is one I have grown myself. Every technique I recommend is something I have tested and used. Every photograph you'll see is one I shot myself. The information you'll find here might not be the newest method or the cleverest trick, but it is 100 percent field-tested and the produce it yields, I believe, has quality.

A word about the title of my book. I am an avid reader and one of the very first books that truly inspired me was Julia Child's landmark book *Mastering the Art of French Cooking.* Not because she lived near us (she did) or because my mom and Julia often bumped into each other at the market (although those are cool stories!), but because Julia knew the value of testing. The best way to understand and then communicate the amazingly complex art of French cooking, she believed, was just to do it. And to keep doing it over and over until you got it just right. Only then would she share what she'd learned with others. I realize there are big differences between French

cooking and vegetable gardening, and I'm not trying to equate myself somehow with Julia Child, who will always be a personal hero of mine. But I think her method was spot on, and it is why her book has been (and continues to be) so successful and so useful to several generations of home cooks.

GARDENING AND HISTORY

As a third-generation gardener living in a house that is now over one hundred years old, I grow plants in the same soil my parents and grandparents did. It's both weird and awesome. This was land that was once plowed by horses, some owned by my ancestors. Old plows are still rusting away against a 250-year-old stone wall in the woods behind us. Having this direct link to history through both genetics and provenance makes me feel connected to the land and the garden in a very real way. And it also points out how much has changed in a couple of generations, as well as how much has not.

I suppose that it might be more romantic if my little homestead was in Vermont or Maine on a nice farm, but the truth is that all of this happened on a very average street in a very average small city in Massachusetts,

which has grown up around us over time. Essentially, my partner of 35 years, Joe, and I garden in what is simply a large city garden located in Worcester, Massachusetts—smack in the middle of USDA Zone 5b. Here, with more elevation than Boston, 30 miles to the east, the summer thunderstorms are fierce as they form in the Berkshires, just 25 miles to the west, while the winters are even fiercer. Worcester is just far away enough from the ocean that it gets frigid in the winter and we get snow that often makes the news. Known as the North Atlantic Snow Belt, a Nor'easter can dump as much as 3 or 4 feet in one storm and over 100 inches a year isn't uncommon.

It's a little amazing to think about the relative that was fed from the old pickling crocks in our cork-lined storeroom in the cellar. But then, as any gardener who lives where other people have gardened knows, an old garden has more weeds that have perennialized, and the soil needs more work in order to keep it fertile. As a gardener, this isn't a bad thing. Our property was a celery farm back in the mid-1800s, so not only do I know that veggies can grow well here, but our soil is that legendary deep loam everyone wants—at least, it is in some parts of

our property. After all, this is New England, and rocks and stone walls are everywhere—a look at the tines on our rototiller will reveal why we often torture-test tillers for rototiller companies.

I've been a gardener my entire life, starting my first veg garden when I was about five with my parents, who were very serious vegetable gardeners their entire lives. My mom was a passionate home canner, or I should say an obsessive one. From about the mid-1930s until the late 1990s, she would can hundreds of quarts of various vegetables, fruits, and mushrooms we had collected from the woods.

Such seasonal living felt normal to my brothers and sister when we were growing up. How could it not? Everything was measured by what season it was in the garden or in the woods. Of course, these seasons also brought out the groans of lazy adolescents like us who sometimes couldn't see the value in days spent picking, skinning, and processing tomatoes outdoors on an open fire, or spreading manure over asparagus beds in the late winter. Today, we blog reverently about it.

GARDENING TODAY

Keeping a vegetable garden today means something very different than it did to our parents, grandparents, or even our great-grandparents. A vegetable garden today doesn't need to fill the freezer or storage room with canned goods. If it does, just a few quarts will suffice (as the Ball canning company seemed to have acknowledged when it revised many of its recipes from 40 to 60 quarts down to 4 to 6 quarts). All of us probably agree that homegrown vegetables are fresher, healthier, and more seasonal than those found even at the local farmers' market. Many of us see the value in farm-to-table cuisine. We actually want to keep bees and make fermented foods and grow our own veggies. This isn't shocking. We live in a world where keeping bees or fermenting sauerkraut doesn't need to be kept secret anymore.

For some reason, many people now associate organic or homegrown vegetables with health, but not with quality. What I mean is that more often than not, a homegrown onion or carrot looks considerably less pretty than its counterparts that were raised on a commercial farm and drenched in chemicals. But just because your carrots are knotted and your potatoes are scabby doesn't mean you have to throw in the towel. That anatomically weird carrot might be a perfect gag to post on Instagram, but it also tastes amazing. We can all do better when it comes to raising vegetables. Yes, the challenges surrounding home gardening persist. Raising thick, crispy celery might and will require far more fertilizer than you probably feel comfortable using. And in the end, the results you achieve aren't always going to be what you had planned. Maybe your celery turned out looking spectacular, but it tasted bitter and dry. Or maybe your fennel bolted, but it produced gorgeous flowers that the pollinators love. We can't control everything, but my greatest hope is that, after you read this book, you will know why things happen like they do and how to better control the things we can—in the garden, at least.

Today, there is more information available on any conceivable topic, and that most definitely includes gardening. Unfortunately, gardening advice can be confusing and is often wrong (this is not a new problem). Home remedies are everywhere, and some do work, but the point is that you really need to know why they work or don't work. This is what I have tried to accomplish with this book.

VARIETY AND RARITY

Another takeaway I hope you get from this book is variety and rarity. The vegetable world has grown exponentially as clever growers and breeders have come up with new cultivars and clever marketers have found new ways to sell them to us. I can remember my dad wondering what kiwi fruit was used for when he first saw them at a market in the 1970s. Today, they are commonplace and no one is confused by them. Take those odd-looking bitter melons and luffa you see at the Asian market. The first time you see them, you'll think they are weird looking, but you'll try them anyway. Or you may decide to grow them; I did. Without knowing anything about them I grew bitter melon for one season, but I did not even know how to tell when they were ripe. I posted pictures of them on my blog, but then the questions poured in: Can you eat the seeds? Are they really bitter? Eventually, I found the answers and today, bitter melon is one of my absolute favorite crops. In this book, you will not only learn how to grow them well, but also what to do after you pick them.

NAVIGATING THIS BOOK

So, here's what this book is not about. It's not about novel methods that make gardening more fun or simple. They may work or not, but I'm not looking for novel. I want to grow the most perfect and healthy vegetables for my kitchen and table. In this book, you aren't going to learn about gardening methods that seem more like diet fads than growing strategies. A good gardening book should offer more than just planting times, optimum soil pH charts, and days-to-maturity data. All that

information can be found today with a simple Internet search. If you are anything like me, your questions tend to be more along the lines of, "Why does my cilantro taste soapier than the bunches I buy at the market?" or, "Why is my zucchini plant not producing as much fruit as my neighbor's?"

This book is about mastery. A resetting or realignment of the how and why we are growing a vegetable garden. It's not your father's vegetable gardening book, but it isn't your "everything is fun and sunny!" gardening book either. I go through the garden vegetable by vegetable, from sowing to harvesting. I discuss what varieties might be worth trying at home, even if you can't find them on the table at your local nursery. I present cultural methods that might seem hard or off-trend at times, but the final choice is up to you.

Heads-up: In *Mastering the Art of Vegetable Gardening*, you will see some inorganic fertilizer suggested. But you will see many completely organic methods suggested as well. You'll find plenty of ways you can adapt useful commercial practices to your home garden, such as using new synthetic mulches and floating row covers, or changing how you time your sowing to avoid insect hatches. I also try to address why some organic methods are just too challenging to maintain at a high and pure level in the small-scale home plot, and I talk about concepts that work reliably, such as pasturing, cover crops, and crop rotation to control insects and disease.

A few final words of advice. What you grow is a personal choice. Be creative. Treat your vegetable garden as your own private fantasy supermarket. Make it the most amazing farming experience you can imagine. Grow things you can't buy at any vegetable stand or find at any store. But also grow the things you use most or find yourself buying every week. Be inspired not to just sow something and let it grow, but to truly master growing it. Make people say, "I can't believe you grew those at home!" In the end, it's all about quality and pleasure. And remember: Gardening is kinda fun! So, let's learn, discover, and master the art of vegetable gardening together.

ONIONS, LEEKS, AND GARLIC

Why are homegrown onions so often small and disappointing? Here's how to grow impressive alliums (hint: the secret to onions is to grow them from seeds).

Onion crops usually disappoint. Garlic frequently does too. At least, that is what I have observed. The problem is almost always the same: most gardeners simply approach onions and garlic too minimally. Take onions, for example. We rake out a nice bed for them in the early spring, buy onion sets or onion plants, and then enjoy planting them in neat, meticulous rows—and that's about the extent of it. A few weeks after planting all may appear fine, as the greens begin to grow and the garden starts to look like a proper vegetable garden. But it's at this crucial point when things start to take a turn for the worse for the overlooked alliums. The onion bulbs just don't seem to get any bigger. For their part, the garlic stalks usually look beautiful, but who knows what is going on underground. We weed, we cultivate, we sprinkle, but the onions never seem to get close to the size you see every day in any corner grocery store. It is a poorly kept secret that most homegrown onions are the size of golf balls when they are finally hoicked from the garden. Tasty, yes, but still underwhelming.

Here is the good news: onions and garlic are actually pretty easy. There is no hidden secret to outshining the alliums at your supermarket. All you need to do is make a couple of modifications to your growing strategy.

STORAGE ONIONS

The onion has a long history as a cultivated food plant, dating back as early as 5000 BC and going back even further into antiquity as a wild-collected edible. Although the wild version bears the botanical Latin name of *Allium cepa*, botanists find it hard to pinpoint where exactly this wild ancestor arose. Most scholars, however, trace cultivated onions to the Iranian peninsula and Iraq, Uzbekistan, and even out toward Mongolia. Onions fed the Egyptian pyramid builders and were included in many burial rituals and tomb paintings. They were even considered sacred by the Egyptians, who believed that the onion had a soul. Columbus brought the onion to the New World around 1492. It quickly spread as a cultivated plant through various indigenous North American tribes, particularly with the Iroquois, who were cultivating onions in what is now New York State in the seventeenth century.

Onions typically are one of the first seed crops planted in midwinter. Seed-raising onions is the preferred method if you want to approach onions seriously. Exhibition growers (who raise onions for state fairs or horticultural exhibitions) all raise their onions from seed.

Home gardeners interested in raising exhibition-type onions are faced with a decision straight out of the gate in midwinter when the seed catalogs arrive. Should you grow your onion crop from seed, from onion sets, or from onion plants? Below you'll find some very straightforward pros and cons for each of these methods.

SEED, SETS, OR PLANTS?

Sets and onion plants often are viewed as easier options, and indeed they are for many home growers. While convenience may be a good reason to use this method, most gardeners will also admit that much of their crop gets harvested on an ongoing basis. So, if it's not your intention to grow onions as storage crops, and you don't mind eating smaller onions, plants or sets may suit your needs just fine.

However, if you want your onions to look like those pictured in seed catalogs, that's another story. If achieving picture-perfect results is your goal, consider not only the method you choose to generate plants (starting from seed is recommended), but also the variety of onion you choose to grow—there are several classes.

SHORT-DAY VERSUS LONG-DAY

Onions can be divided into two groups. Think of short-day onions as sweet onions with a limited shelf life, and think of long-day onions as storage onions with a hotter flavor. Cooks are familiar with these definitions, as the two groups of onions are used for different purposes in the kitchen. The 'Vidalia' types or "sweet onions" can

OPPOSITE: Onions must be cured or air-dried for a few days before storing.

LEFT: Onions require heavy fertility and plenty of water to grow large. **CENTER:** Cell-raised onion seedling ready to plant. **RIGHT:** 'Bianca di Maggio' is an uncommon Italian heirloom cipollini onion.

be eaten like apples. They have a higher water content, are less flavorful, and often are used raw in salads. They have a limited season, however, and are not good keepers.

But let's say that your garden is in a cold climate, and you want to raise sweet onions like the 'Walla Walla Sweets' or the 'Vidalia' types. These short-day onions are specially bred for growing in warm climates as a winter crop, so even though you can find seeds or seedlings of these varieties for northern gardens, they are not recommended if you expect to get a market-type product. If you plant these varieties in a cold climate, you will still get harvestable onions, but they will be smaller and hotter than you might expect.

What is the actual difference between short-day and long-day onions? Part of it is purely chemical, and part of it is physiological, defined by day length and air temperature. For example, sweet onions raised in soils low in sulfur or calcium are often hotter, whereas warm growing conditions paired with long summer day length will result in a completely different product. Sweet onions are primarily intended for those raising winter crops in the warmer parts of the planet. The variety names provide hints as to their ideal growing region. A 'Walla Walla Sweet' must then come from Washington State in a region near Walla Walla. The same clues are provided by the famed 'Vidalia' onion, and the 'Georgia Sweet', 'Texas Sweet', and 'Maui Sweet' onions.

NOTE: You will find many sweet onion varieties sold in seed catalogs as bundles of pre-started plants available even to northern gardeners. These were raised in a previous season, as with onion sets, and then carefully stored. The trick is to know what you are buying and recognize how appropriate the variety is for your area. Long-day and short-day onions require different growing conditions. Long-day (or storage onions) need 14 or more hours of sunlight per day. Short-day varieties grow best in mild climates where the days are short (areas below the 35th parallel), and these varieties cannot tolerate hard freezes.

RAISING ONIONS FROM SEED

The finest onion crops are raised from seed. The process is rather low-maintenance if the seeds are grown under lights or on a heating mat on a porch. The tricks are simple—start very early in the season (late January through February for most) and then transplant into larger cells before setting the seedlings out into the garden.

The difference between seed-raised onions and those from onions sets is enormous at harvest, but it's not something apparent in the spring. A month after planting, comparing a bed of emerging onion sets to a bed of onion seedlings can be disappointing, but compare them two months later and you'll get a completely different story. Seed-raised plants will establish more roots, grow without stress, and remain growing longer than either sets or pre-started plants. Sow seeds individually into plug trays, or in rows in seed flats, as onions can handle transplanting well. Seed guides offered by large seed companies may suggest direct sowing, but while this method is often used by farms, they also use herbicide to keep weed growth to a minimum. Home-started seedlings are preferred because it is difficult to control weed competition with direct-sown seed—onion seedlings are very small, often confused with grass seedlings, and are easily outcompeted.

Seedlings will progress slowly at first, looking more like grass than anything else for the first month or two. If growing under artificial light, make every attempt to keep the atmosphere cool (60°F), to slow down growth. Some growers trim back the seedlings with scissors if they grow too lanky or tall. Be sure to cut the top few inches only, and not the growing point lower on the seedling.

Fertilize seedlings biweekly once they emerge with a balanced 10-10-10 water-soluble feed to keep them growing without stress. The onion plants can be set out into the garden after a week of being hardened off (brought outdoors during the day) to become sturdy and acclimated. This can be as early as mid-April in Zone 6, and as late as May in cold climates. Properly hardened onion plants can handle light frosts.

Onions raised from seedlings or onion sets both require a similar treatment once set out into the garden: proper nutrition to meet their high demands for fertility (especially nitrogen and sulfur) as well as a continual supply of water. Onions perform best with no mulch and when beds are kept well weeded.

ONIONS IN THE FIELD

Onions are bulbs, or *geophytes*, and as such have some unique demands. With onions, it's not about the quality of the leaf or the fruit, and you don't need to care about pollination or fruit set. This is a crop that is all about forming a high-quality bulb, which is demanding both biologically for the plant and culturally for us.

Nitrogen. Onions are a high-nitrogen crop, but they also need relatively high phosphorus and potassium. They are one of the few vegetables for which frequent application of all three elements is required. But mostly, they need high nitrogen—in fact, they may be the most nitrogen-needy crop in the garden. Since nitrogen is not long-lived in the soil, it must be added frequently.

Because onions have shallow roots you may use slower-acting organic sources, such as feather meal or fish meal. Poultry manure and urea are also strong sources. Some organic growers have been known to triple or quadruple the suggested application amounts when fertilizing onions which is unheard of for any other crop. I should mention that plants don't recognize a difference between the various sources of nitrogen available to the home gardener. As far as they are concerned, nitrogen is nitrogen, and whether it came from corn, a byproduct of the petroleum industry, or the butt of a chicken, it's still nitrogen.

Commercial farmers apply conventional fertilizer by side-dressing with a granular product high in nitrogen every 30 days. They may use high-ratio products with at least 40-0-0 of ammonium sulfate or ammonium nitrate. You can buy these for yourself at farm stores or online, but a safer bet might be to invest in some composted manure from an organic farm or use granular urea, a rare mineral called Langbeinite (if applied in winter as it is slow to release) or feather meal in addition to manure. Serious growers who exhibit onions at county fairs often double up on both a granular 15-15-15 from the start and add additional 30-percent-strength nitrogen and potassium during the height of the growing season.

Stop the feeding phases approximately 4 weeks before harvest. Excess nitrogen applied too late will delay maturity and can cause onions to have thick necks, which renders them useless as storage onions.

Weeding. Onion beds do require weeding as onion quality often suffer with mulches. Well-tended onion beds always look beautiful when they are impeccably groomed. European gardeners seem to know this, as rarely do you see an untidy or mulched onion bed in Germany or Switzerland. A bed of neatly grown and well-tended onions in rows does have its merits—it's a fine way to show off your agricultural skills and demonstrate that you can have success without relying on chemical herbicides.

Watering. Given the high moisture content of an onion, it should come as no surprise that frequent watering is essential when raising onions. A daily sprinkling is ideal during the hottest weeks in midsummer, especially during dry spells—even more so if you are raising onions from sets, as these can bolt and go to seed if overstressed. If you live in a water-restricted area, it might make sense to use a drip hose system, grow some in large containers, or skip growing onions altogether. Many exhibition onion growers in England grow their giant onions in large pots.

Lastly, while great for children's science projects, resist planting old onions that have started sprouting in the kitchen. These may provide some early greens, but they will never grow into onions again, as onions are biennial, and the bulb's energy at this phase will be directed into producing a flower stem and seed.

UNCOMMON ONION VARIETIES YOU SHOULD KNOW

Negi-Style Onions. 'Negi' or Negi-style onions essentially are larger scallions than typically found in the West. Very choice and select, Negi-style green onions are highly sought after by specialty cooks and are especially valued in Japan, where the art of raising them began.

Negi-style onions are a crop most people won't encounter unless they live near a large Asian market, but they are very useful in the kitchen, as they bridge the gap between a leek and a green onion. In the home garden, many green onion varieties can be raised "Negi-style" by starting seeds indoors in individual pots, and then transplanting them outside so the onions can grow uncrowded and become taller and thicker. A good fertilizer program high in nitrogen is key, as well as plenty of consistent moisture, along with cool weather.

Negi-style onions are best raised as a fall crop in short-season areas, set out into the garden in July and tended throughout the summer before harvesting them in autumn. They are rarely seen outside of Japan, but many varieties of green onion seeds are suitable for Negi-style culture, as they are the same varieties sold in Japan. It makes for a fun summer project for the more adventurous foodie and grower.

GROWING GREEN ONIONS (SCALLIONS)

Often overlooked as a garden crop, green onions are one of the most sensible crops to grow. If you seem to buy a bunch or two of green onions every time you go to the store, it probably makes sense to try your hand at growing your own. The only problem with growing green onions is that very few of us know how to grow them well.

Green onions are never sold as seedlings or as pre-started plants, and freshly picked green onions are superior than any store-bought variety, especially to the home chef, as you can slice them razor-thin because the foliage is far more tender but isn't crushed nor wilted. The varieties available from seed are nearly endless, including reds, purples, white-shanked, and many Japanese or Negi-types. Like all onions, green onions are easy to

VARIETIES

LONG-DAY STORAGE ONIONS

'Yankee'—A mildew-resistant yellow storage onion that can be stored up to 6 months.

'Ailsa Craig' open-pollinated (110 days)— An heirloom for culture in 38°–60° latitudes. It's an old variety believed to be a cross between 'Danvers Yellow' and 'Cranston's Excelsior'. Introduced in 1887, it is commonly grown in England as a large exhibition type.

'Patterson' F1 hybrid (104 days)—An excellent storage onion similar to 'Copra', but with higher yields and better disease resistance. Adapted for culture between 38°–55° latitudes.

'Cortland'—A big yellow storage onion with a skinnier neck that is easier to braid.

'Redwing'—A long-storage red onion.

'Monastrell'—A red onion with flattened bulbs that can grow large. Known for its quality and uniform red color throughout all the rings. Late season.

'Red Long of Tropea'—An heirloom Italian red onion with an elegant long-shaped bulb. Not good for storage, but grown as a fresh bunching onion for late-summer harvests.

INTERMEDIATE OR DAY-NEUTRAL TYPES

'Scout'—An early yellow or Spanish onion classified as an intermediate day-length option suitable for growing in northern or southern climates. More disease-resistant, it forms large onions. Stored onions last 3 to 4 months.

'Sierra Blanca'—All-America Selections (AAS) winner. White, big, and of high quality. Storage onion for long-day culture in cold climates, or fall-sown as a short-day culture in warm climates.

SWEET ONIONS—SHORT-DAY

'Gabriella'—A yellow short-day type that is more bolt-resistant and forms nice, round bulbs in areas where onions are planted in the fall.

'Walla Walla'—A classic short-day variety for late-summer sowing in areas where sweet onions can be grown all winter and harvested early the following summer. Elsewhere it can be raised as a choice green or spring onion, or as a slightly smaller yet juicier summer onion in cold climates.

SPECIALTY ONIONS

'Gold Coin'—A yellow cipollini type (small, flattened bulbs) better for growing in cold climates as a long-day onion than other cipollini types. This one stores better than 'Bianca di Maggio'.

'Bianca di Maggio'—An all-white, cipollini-type onion, it has small, flattened bulbs with green tops. For specialty markets or as classic flat cipollini onions from the home garden. Best raised as a winter crop in mild areas, as with other short-day types.

Many old heirloom pass-along onions such as 'Egyptian onions' (walking onions) are common in old gardens and are often the first greens harvested in the spring; however, most are not useful in the kitchen except while very immature.

'Welsh Onion'—*Allium fistulosum*—Fistulosum means "hollow stem." While there are many named or pass-along cultivars of *A. fistulosum* including red-stalked and many white-stalked forms, all share common traits as each are easy-to-grow, long-lived perennial onions.

'Egyptian Onion'—Old-fashioned pass-along plant. Top-setting (it forms small onion clusters on the tops of stems that often have bulbous bases). Useful for some, and just nostalgic for others, this perennial onion has tender greens in the spring and beautiful white flower stalks.

'Yellow Multiplier'—Winter-hardy bulbs form clusters by autumn, which is when you should look for them in catalogs. Often hard to find—best to find a friend who has them to share.

germinate and to grow—if you sow them at the right time and care for them. Call them scallions, green onions, bunching onions, or spring onions, they are all relatively the same when it comes to growing.

Planting Green Onions. Green onions started from seed should be directly sown into a prepared bed in early spring, around the same time you plant radishes. Onion seeds are large enough to allow you to sprinkle them sparsely in a band about 3 inches wide. Plant the entire length of the bed, as you will be harvesting them from one end to the other to make room for other crops, such as radishes. Strive for a seed spacing of about ½ inch to 1 inch, which may seem thick, but remember—these are green onions, and you won't be allowing them to grow any thicker than ¼ inch in diameter before harvesting. This is when they are at their very best quality. Cover the seeds with ¼ inch of soil and water well, being sure to label the row as emergence can be slow. Some gardeners like to sow a few radish seeds along with the green onions to identify the row, but I find that this sometimes ruins the symmetry and spacing of the green onions.

The most difficult thing about raising green onions is to leave the seed bed alone for as long as possible. Also be sure to monitor weed growth—baby green onions look very much like grass for the first weeks of their lives. Thinning is unnecessary unless you've overseeded, but normally you want a crowd when raising green onions.

Harvesting. Green onions can be harvested very young if you wish. They are now commonly grown as microgreens, but they are better for most dishes once they start forming white bases on the plants. They last remarkably long in the garden, so you can harvest over a long period of time. In cold climates, rows sown at the end of March can start to be harvested by mid-May, lasting through the salad season of early June until July. A second and a third crop can be sown starting at the end of June and again around the first week of July, providing continual harvests of green onions until the coldest autumn weather arrives. Fancy Japanese varieties are better for autumn crops. Sow these in late July, and monitor watering to make sure they never dry out. These varieties are sought after by many home cooks. They look very similar to leeks with long, white stems, but are much more tender and can be used raw. When green onions cost over a dollar a bunch, having an endless supply is a luxury any cook would relish.

LEEKS
Allium porrum

While leeks share some rather close genetics with onions (both are alliums and botanically considered bulbs or geophytes), the leek is known to be much older and closer to the wild species *Allium ampeloprasum*—considered to be the great-grandparent of most of the culinary alliums we eat today.

Leeks are really the closest thing genetically to elephant garlic (which isn't a true garlic by the way). This isn't just a random plant fact, but one worth understanding if you want to grow leeks well. Leek growing culture is significantly different than the conditions recommended for garlic or conventional onions.

Leeks take great skill to grow well. In England, raising prize-winning leeks is practically a national sport, but in North America many of us have never even bought leeks at the market. In the garden, leeks are a responsive crop that can impress. Old varieties were knighted with cultivar names like 'Giant Musselburgh' and 'Bulgarian Giant', and today new varieties called 'Megaton' and 'Hannibal' still rule. In truth, most leeks were simply named after the region where they were originally grown or selected and not for their size, but I like to think there might be a leek variety in the future called Boeing 787 or Optimus Prime. Home cooks won't care,

though, because leeks are valued for their mild, oniony flavor and buttery texture.

Leeks are an old-fashioned crop. The yellow French leek 'Jaune du Poitou', a leek introduced by M. Vilmorin in 1853, is considered by many to be the finest heirloom variety sometimes still available in seed exchanges, with immense foliage that can reach amazing lengths of nearly 5 feet long. Most leeks are white-stalked with pale green centers and are long-lasting in the garden, as they can be covered in straw and harvested throughout the winter.

The value of the leek, particularly in early America, was closely associated with this winter hardiness, which allowed it to withstand mild winters still out in the field—essential before refrigeration. In North America, particularly in the Northeast, the 'Musselburgh' types were grown along with French types and all leeks were essential as fresh winter vegetables. They often appear in recipes along with other winter veggies like potatoes and cabbage for this reason.

GROWING LEEKS

As with storage onions, the finest leeks come from seed. Leeks are one of the earliest vegetables you need to get going. Even in cold climates, seed must be started by early February. In Great Britain, France, and Scotland, leeks can be started still earlier, or even in the autumn or early winter if you have a cold frame or greenhouse. Sow your

OPPOSITE: Leeks are set out much like onions as seedlings in early spring.

leeks in individual cell containers or pots 4 to 6 inches wide. Most of us will do fine with 2- to 4-inch cell containers and a sterile soilless mix. Sow two or three seeds into each, covering them with ¼ inch of soil. As with onions, you can sow seed thicker and thin the seedlings when transplanting out into the garden.

Bottom heat near 75°F is ideal for keeping the soil warm, but just until germination, after which you should move the trays to a slightly cooler area (near 65°F). Leek seed is easy to germinate. Once seedlings emerge, move the seed trays or cell containers under grow lights where it is cooler, or even better, into a cool greenhouse. Like onions, leek seedlings must be fed a steady diet of nitrogen as they are heavy feeders. A balanced liquid feed (10-10-10) at half strength is recommended until plants go into the garden. Fungus gnats and green slime can form on seedling trays with this additional feed, but frequent drying out between watering will reduce problems. The goal with leeks is to get seedlings as thick as a pencil by mid-April before planting them. When planting time comes, leeks require depth when set into the garden so that they can develop their long white necks. Plants should be set down deep into trenches, which must be dug 6 to 8 inches deep. Soil can be pulled in around the growing leeks over the next month until only the tops are emerging. Leeks form a nice, white stalk and the portion that remains underground will be the most tender when harvested. Leeks, like onions, demand fertile soil starting with granular phosphorus in early spring, followed by monthly amending with granular sidedressing of both nitrogen and potassium (20-5-10).

Blanching. As the leek seedlings grow, soil should be hilled-up around their stalks. By protecting them from sunlight, you will blanch the primary stalks, which are the tastiest part of leeks. As with onions, leeks must never be mulched. However, you do need to weed enthusiastically to keep the plants growing.

Harvesting. Leeks are best kept in the ground until after the first frost, when they are said to develop a sweeter flavor. Old New England farmers would store loose blankets of straw over the beds, keeping the soil frost-free all winter, and leeks could be harvested until spring. Because they are true biennials (like garlic and onions), leeks will stay through to the second year, when they will bloom and set seed.

OPPOSITE: Seedling leeks are some of the first seeds sown. **ABOVE LEFT:** Plant leeks deep into the soil to produce long, white stalks. **ABOVE RIGHT:** Late fall leeks ready to be dug.

VARIETIES

'King Richard' open-pollinated (75 days)—Sometimes sold as bundled leek plants in the spring, which can give northern gardeners a boost, it's a full-sized variety that can withstand hard frost and freezes in the winter.

'Pandora' open-pollinated (90 days)—An earlier-maturing leek that's good for late-summer to early fall harvests. Produces a longer white shank compared to other varieties.

'Megaton' F1 hybrid (90 days)—Beautiful upright plants that offer premium high-yield results for CSAs and home gardeners. Forms thick shanks.

'Bandit' open-pollinated (120 days)—Some of the nicest dark bluish-green foliage on any leek, with a very thick shank.

GARLIC

Allium sativum var. *ophioscorodon*

A. SATIVUM VAR. SATIVUM

Plain obsession. That's maybe the clearest way to describe those who love and grow garlic. Aside from chili peppers, few crops have such a following. Its fans attend garlic festivals, celebrate the annual harvest, and share recipes that maximize what makes garlic so addictive. Of course, it does have its haters. Nevertheless, garlic has a long and storied history punctuated with myriad uses both medicinal and culinary.

As a garden plant, garlic is surprisingly easy to grow and very productive. It has the added benefit of filling a season (autumn through spring) when many beds lie fallow, as garlic cloves must be planted in the autumn (like tulips) and harvested in early to mid-summer. Garlic is also a stately plant in the garden. Every phase of its growth is attractive. Garlic varieties can show growth soon after planting in the autumn, although some wait until first thing in the spring. Garlic scapes, the flower buds, must be removed before flowering but are beautiful as they begin to appear in early summer. They have several uses in the kitchen, including picking for a summer treat.

GROWING GARLIC

Without looking too hard, you can find dozens of varieties of garlic suited for home growing. Seed

OPPOSITE: Garlic scapes sprout from each plant in late spring and should be cut off to allow the plant to focus energy on the garlic bulbs.

purveyors often catalog their garlic varieties by type—hardneck and softneck— and then tell a bit of the backstory behind each variety, which is often as interesting as that of any heirloom tomato. The most difficult thing for gardeners to remember is exactly when to order garlic, as it is shipped during their brief dormant period in late summer until early autumn. The ideal time for most gardeners to sow their garlic sets is in late autumn.

Garlic will arrive as garlic heads—much as you'd find garlic at the supermarket. Upon arrival or purchase, open the boxes immediately and separate the cloves from the main bulb by carefully peeling each clove away from the central stalk (if it is hardneck garlic). Hardnecks will still have their woody central stem. Softneck garlic does not have as large a central stem, so peeling it is more like peeling grocery store garlic, which is normally softneck.

GARLIC VARIETIES

Garlic can be divided into two main groups: hardneck (Rocambole or top-setting garlic) and softneck (or braiding garlic). The "neck" refers to the central stem found standing at the end of the season. Softneck types allow you to braid the garlic and are the most common type of garlic commercially. Hardneck types form a very hard stem and are popular with collectors and growers who believe these types are stronger flavored, store better, and produce cloves that are easier to peel.

Botanically, hardneck and softneck types have been divided into two distinct subspecies: *Allium sativum* var. *ophioscorodon*, which includes the hardneck types, and *A. sativum* var. *sativum*, which includes the softneck types. Each is worth growing if you've never grown garlic, as the crops are immensely useful in the kitchen, and it's fun to have a variety of different types of garlic to experiment with.

Within these two subgroups are other divisions. Softneck garlic can be further divided into two other type-groups—one called silverskin-type and the other artichoke-type. These definitions describe the overall bulb formation. Artichoke types are much larger and often are more productive in the garden, and each head can form many cloves, yet the inner cloves can be smaller.

Silverskin types are what most people are familiar with, as these are more commonly found at local supermarkets. They typically form cloves that are white-

Order garlic sets by midsummer for sowing in October, as garlic cloves need time to root, if not grow, a bit before hard freezes occur.

skinned and more uniform in shape. These types also don't form flower stalks as hardneck types will. The cloves can be harder to separate from the main head, but the varieties are often more attractive and easier to braid. Silverskin softnecks are better varieties for warmer climates. Purple-tinted varieties from eastern Europe tend to be the hottest and most flavorful, but it is difficult to claim that one variety is any better than another.

I should mention a third garlic type here, commonly sold as elephant garlic. It is a completely different species—*Allium ampeloprasum*. Not botanically a garlic, it still has a similar, very mild flavor, but it is not the same plant. It's worth planting if just for its spectacular beauty.

PLANTING GARLIC

Like the onion, garlic prefers a neutral soil pH, from 6.5 to 7.0. Also like the onion, it is a heavy feeder. If you want large, healthy garlic bulbs, you will need fertilizer. The most common mistake home growers make is to assume that because garlic is a bulb it doesn't need food. Garlic might look completely healthy when growing in the garden, but what you see is above ground. Pleasing, but you really want to encourage the bulb formation underground.

Good garlic yields depend on starting with high phosphorus in the soil as with any bulb plant. A fertilizer in the 5-10-5 range is good, as it offers an additional kick of nitrogen and potassium along with higher phosphorus. Sprinkle a ½ cup into an 8-foot trench just below where the garlic will be planted, then cover with an inch of soil before planting.

This should hold the plants through the winter, as some will sprout in autumn and others in spring. There will be plenty of root action, however. As soon as the plants emerge in early spring, side-dress another ½ cup along each side, 3 inches next to the emerging growth. Continue to add through midsummer and then stop a month before harvest (in July in most of North America), as an excess of nitrogen during bulb formation can affect bulb size negatively.

While the nitrogen needs of garlic are higher than other vegetables, they are not as extreme as that of onions. An organic source, often fish-based, will be adequate. Look for 5-0-0 or higher.

Fall planting. Traditionally, garlic is planted in the fall—this allows the bulbs to form roots and establish themselves much like other autumn-planted bulbs. The ideal time in the autumn depends on where you live. In the Central Atlantic, this may be as early as mid-October, but it can be as late as November. In cold climates, plant garlic just as the leaves are changing and before hard frosts freeze the ground. Some garlic varieties will begin growing foliage almost immediately after planting so don't be alarmed to see green growth starting in November. The plants will be fine.

Spring planting. Garlic can be planted in the early spring. Just store the bulbs in a cool, dry environment that is below 40°F for at least 4 weeks. If vernalizing in a refrigerator, be careful, as apples or anything producing

VARIETIES

There are dozens and dozens of varieties, including fascinating heirlooms. Instead of listing the many varieties of garlic, I'll just outline the various types and set you on your journey. When searching for varieties, note their flavor profile, which can range from mild to scorching-hot.

HARDNECK TYPES
Purple Stripe Group—Purple-striped cloves often with strong garlic flavor. Midseason.
Porcelain Group—Large bulbs with pure-white, papery skins. Late.
Rocambole Group—Cloves with loose papery skins and brownish flesh. Midseason.
SOFTNECK TYPES
Artichoke Group—The most common garlic found in supermarkets. White skin. Early to midseason.
Silverskin Group—Long-keeping storage type with very mild flavor. Late.

ABOVE: Freshly dug hardstem garlic before curing. **OPPOSITE:** Immature garlic plants.

ethylene gas can affect the bulbs' ability to sprout. Crops planted in the spring may be slower to emerge, and harvest will be delayed by a couple of weeks.

Maintenance. Garlic prefers not to be mulched. Hand-weeding is best. Moisture is essential, and a constant supply will ensure that you get a premium yield of big garlic heads. Water early in the day or use a drip irrigation system to help maintain consistency. Garlic scapes will appear in early summer and must be cut or snapped off to allow the garlic to focus on forming bulbs. The scapes are usually beautiful but should not be allowed to bloom. Snap them off just as they are developing flower buds.

Harvesting. Garlic is ready to pick when the tops have begun to fade in midsummer. The ideal moment to dig plants to dry is while some green leaves remain on the plant. Experienced growers dig garlic just as the bottom ⅓ of the leaves have started to fade, not when the plant is completely dried out. Leaving plants in the soil too long is a common error. The problem is largely cosmetic, but if you want pure white, unblemished skins, then be sure to dig the entire plant and bulb just as they begin to fade.

If the weather has been exceptionally dry, water the bed deeply a day before digging to help plump up the garlic. You will notice that the bulbs have lush root systems when first dug out of the ground—this is natural. Don't trim the tops or roots until the plants have been curing and drying for a month. After pulling, do not rinse the bulbs. Let them dry in open shade until evening, when they should be brought indoors to a warm and dry spot where they will be allowed to cure for a couple of months. Take great care not to damage the bulbs as it will cause them to decay. You can cut the hard stems to half their length for the first month, and then cut them shorter if you wish.

ASPARAGUS, RHUBARB, AND ARTICHOKES

The annual ritual of tilling fresh earth and planting new seeds is at the core of our love for gardening. But in some cases it is unnecessary, and that's good too. A well-established bed of productive perennials offers edibles that arrive year after year with minimal effort from the gardeners who grow them. Among vegetable growers, the most common perennials are asparagus, rhubarb, and artichoke. While not related by anything other than their perennialness, all three of these plants require similar planting and maintenance.

ASPARAGUS

There is much to be said about asparagus in the garden. While it requires an investment in space and some time up front, it's often the first crop you can harvest every spring, and the quality of freshly picked asparagus cannot be matched.

The genus *Asparagus* is large, with more than 300 species, some of them ornamental and commonly used as houseplants or as decorative garden plants. A diverse genus, it includes tropical vines, desert plants, and some species that form tubers. Only one species, however, is considered edible: *Asparagus officinalis*, which is commonly referred to as simply "asparagus."

Asparagus is an old vegetable believed to be of Persian origin. Its origin remains mysterious, as even in the earliest recorded history the plant had been naturalized throughout Europe and the Mediterranean. In fact, one of Emperor Augustus's favorite sayings was "Citius quam asparagi coquentur," which translates as "Do it quicker than you can cook asparagus."

An asparagus bed in the garden today is very much like a retirement account. The longer the roots sit in the garden, the better the crop becomes. Well-planted asparagus will deliver dividends throughout a lifetime or two. You can find asparagus beds in New England that

were planted in the late nineteenth century, and many multigenerational family homes keep such legacy beds (including mine). Continued growth and high yields requires annual maintenance to maintain a rich soil.

Finding a place for asparagus in a contemporary garden can be a challenge, as gardening styles have changed—especially over the past 50 years. In the 1940s, asparagus might be found planted in wide trenches along the far end of a large vegetable garden, where it could remain undisturbed.

Home gardeners today are often limited in space and have much less leisure time than did their parents, and even less time than their postwar grandparents, who dutifully kept a Victory Garden, usually edged with a few rows of asparagus. Younger gardeners are much more likely to grow asparagus in a dedicated bed, preferably not a raised bed (because it may decay before the plants reach maturity). Mulches like straw or hay will ease some of the care issues, but avoid using wood bark or plastic.

Asparagus will grow in a container, but it is hardly worth the effort as roots can grow 6 feet deep and you need at least 24 plants to be able to harvest a meaningful crop (producing a handful of spears every few days). As you will learn, there are simply no shortcuts when it comes to raising asparagus. Thankfully, it's a long-lived plant once established in the garden.

OPPOSITE: Contrary to common opinion, 'Purple Passion' is not an heirloom variety at all but rather a 1990 tetraploid.

ABOVE AND OPPOSITE: A new asparagus bed is a long-term investment, so choose a sunny site carefully. Prepare the soil with plenty of manure and compost deeply turned-in. Two-year-old crowns should be soaked in water for a couple hours and then set in at the same depth as when they were growing to allow new sprouts to emerge. A new bed will start bearing sizable stalks within 2 years and will bear increasing yields for nearly 20 years.

VARIETIES

'Early Argenteuil' (Precoce D'Argenteuil), 1885—An early forcing variety, also commonly used for forcing white spears under straw.

'Connover's Colossal', 1870s—Thick-stemmed heirloom variety that must be raised from seed but is very choice.

'Crimson Pacific'—A purple variety that is tender and high-yielding.

'Mary Washington', 1949—A very popular mid-twentieth-century variety that performs well in the garden. Dark-green spears.

HARVESTING YOUR ASPARAGUS

Although tempting, resist harvesting the new beds of asparagus for at least 2 years and often 3. Allow the ferny growth to grow tall to encourage healthy root formation. Expect your first light harvest to come in year 3 then grow larger every year after that. Contrary to what many believe, thicker asparagus spears are better than thin, and these come from mature plants that are properly maintained. Thinner spears are often tougher and more fibrous, and tend to come from plants that are poorly grown, in deep shade or not properly fertilized.

Asparagus season is short and weather-dependent. Spears will begin emerging in late winter or early spring, depending on where you live. Tight spears must be hand-cut each day, as tips emerge and grow quickly. Snap them off at the point where the stems are tender, or cut them carefully just below the surface of the ground, taking care not to hit newly emerging shoots.

After 4 weeks the season will be over, signified by shoots that elongate quickly, seemingly overnight. While still edible, it's best to allow these spears to mature, growing into tall, waving wands of ferny foliage. Through the summer, maintain the bed as weed-free as you can.

RHUBARB

Rhubarb is one of the most beloved of old-fashioned vegetables. While many consider it a fruit, it's the petiole of the leaf that we eat; furthermore, it is grown in or alongside the vegetable garden and is sold with vegetables, so it fits firmly within the vegetable category. Along with another perennial vegetable crop, asparagus, rhubarb shares a similar culture.

HOW TO GROW RHUBARB

It's true that rhubarb is easy to grow, perhaps the easiest and most long-lived of all vegetables, but a little attention before planting the dormant roots will ensure a long life and annual harvests of the bright red stems so useful in jams, jellies, and pie filling.

Rhubarb enjoys rich soil, consistent moisture, and full sun, although partial shade will not harm it. The ideal site should be well thought out, as once plants are set into the ground they may stay there for 20 years or more. Even though they are long-lived, to help plants maintain vigor it is recommended to lift and divide plants every 5 years. This will result in divisions you can share or use to extend a row.

A family of four will only need a short row or two of rhubarb, perhaps six plants positioned on the far end of a vegetable plot near the asparagus, as they are both perennial crops. Keeping the two crops as neighbors will help you navigate a tiller through the garden in the spring. You can start certain varieties of rhubarb from seed, but it is much easier to order root stock, which is shipped while dormant in the early spring. Nurseries will know the proper time to ship roots.

Dig-in aged manure to a depth of 2 feet. Make certain the soil is rich with organic matter, be it leaf litter, humus, or compost. When plants arrive, soak the roots for a couple of hours and then position the crowns so only the buds or tips are emerging from the soil. Ideally, the crowns should be set 1 inch below the surface of the soil. They will self-adjust through the summer to the ideal height so that the rounded cobs can emerge in the spring which will unfold spectacularly into giant leaves and stalks. Rhubarb makes a magnificent plant, but be forewarned—the foliage is large, and even one plant can consume at least 9 square feet.

Maintenance is easy. Plan on harvesting stalks until mid-July, but always allow the plant to continue thriving by keeping a few leaves on the plant. You can harvest rhubarb later, but you should stop by midsummer to allow the plants to regain strength for the winter.

Flower stems will begin to emerge by the end of June, but these should be cut off at their base so the plant can conserve energy, focusing it on root and foliage growth. Rhubarb is a welcome sight in any garden, and its rather maintenance-free habit will annually reward the gardener with plenty of stalks for years to come.

NOTE: The leaves of rhubarb contain oxalate crystals and anthraquinones (glycosides), which are toxic if consumed in large quantities. When harvesting, remove the leaf and perhaps an inch or so of the petiole (stalk) leading to it just to be safe.

RHUBARB VARIETIES

There are many varieties of rhubarb available, but you may need to look hard to find them. Varieties vary in size and in stalk diameter, length, and color. Some are completely red inside and out, while others are speckled or entirely green. Most varieties are difficult to source, however, as the most common commercial variety is 'Victoria'. It is worth seeking out unusual or rare types, as the plants are long-lived.

BELOW: Perennial rhubarb plants are among the first greens to emerge in spring and herald the coming gardening season.
OPPOSITE: 'McDonald's Canadian Red' rhubarb produces stems nearly as thick as a man's wrist.

VARIETIES

'Victoria'—The classic variety with dark-pink stalks.

'Timperley Early'—A British variety, it is typically planted in the autumn and is the premium variety for forcing in January (which is popular in the United Kingdom).

'Colorado Red'—One of the few all-red varieties—very choice, as the red color continues throughout the stalk.

'Fraulein Sharfer Torte'—A premium all-red German variety; one of the best.

'Stockbridge Arrow'—A deep red variety with thick stems up to 24 inches long, and arrow-shaped leaves. Considered highly ornamental.

'Holstein Bloodred'—Very dark red stalks that are good for canning and freezing.

'German Wine'—A lovely and unusual rhubarb with green stems that are speckled with red.

ARTICHOKES

I like to use the analogy of cooks versus bakers when providing advice on annual artichoke culture. The fact is that artichoke culture isn't exactly easy, especially outside of areas where a Mediterranean climate favors their culture.

The globe artichoke (not to be confused with the Jerusalem artichoke, a tuberous relative of the sunflower) is a large, attractive, thistlelike plant with sharp spines and silvery leaves. Humans have been eating the immature large flower buds or heads since biblical times, and while scholars cannot agree on the origin of the plant, most believe that it likely was introduced by the Arabs into Europe. While the globe artichoke came to the United States in the late seventeenth century (Thomas Jefferson grew it at Monticello), it wasn't until 1920, when Italian immigrants brought the 'Green Globe' variety to California, that the artichoke became a significant agricultural crop.

For nearly a century, if a home gardener wanted to raise globe artichokes, they had to purchase root stock, vegetative divisions, or potted nursery plants. The market was limited, and most home growers experienced disappointing results. The reasons for failure were often simple. Artichokes cannot survive in soil that drops below 25°F, and as a true perennial, it requires at least 2 years before plants produce buds. Hardy and robust in the proper climate, there are fields of 'Green Globe' ar-

OPPOSITE: Globe artichoke.

tichokes over 80 years old, but for the most part, it remained overlooked in the home vegetable garden.

Everything changed in the mid-1990s, when plant breeding efforts in California developed an entirely new way to raise perennial artichokes. Still botanically perennial, new varieties could now be grown in a single growing season as an annual crop. Practically overnight, commercial farmers and even home gardeners could grow globe artichokes of very fine quality from seed, with no worries about wintering over.

Before undertaking all the work required, I must be honest about a couple of significant points. First, a healthy, mature artichoke plant can be too large for most raised beds. If you are thinking about raising one in a pot, the truth is that it sulks as a container plant. If an artichoke plant finds itself in a challenging environment, it will only produce leaves and appear stunted— lovely foliage, but nothing to eat.

The second point is perhaps the greatest disappointment first-time growers discover. A single plant will produce only one or two full-sized globe artichokes. So, you should evaluate the investment in time and energy before undertaking an artichoke program. While it's true that secondary buds will emerge from side branches, they will be considerably smaller (but equally delicious). I often pull my plants before this happens, and you may wish to do so as well in order to save space for late-season crops.

Globe artichokes are best suited for the larger vegetable garden—a few dozen plants should be enough to keep any cook happy. Even with all this fuss, for the hardcore artichoke fan, nothing beats a homegrown bud.

CHOOSING THE RIGHT VARIETY

Annual crops begin with sourcing the seed of varieties bred for annual production. While still botanically considered perennial, these are varieties that respond well to techniques like vernalization (a period where young seedlings are exposed to a brief chilling), which will stimulate the plants to produce large, full-sized buds of high quality.

The flagship annual variety for such annual treatment is 'Imperial Star', the result of an extensive breeding program at the University of California–Irvine, during the late 1980s. Introduced into the trade in 1992, 'Imperial Star' forever changed annual artichoke production, opening a new niche market for growers by offering a variety that produces large, high-quality buds.

Most home gardeners will be limited as to what varieties they can grow from seed in the annual method, with three varieties recommended for North American gardeners ('Imperial Star', 'Northern Star', and 'Emerald'). If you live in a traditional artichoke-growing area, there are many selections that offer benefits from being regionally unique to those considered culturally significant.

The classic commercial variety found in supermarkets is 'Green Globe'. An 'Improved Green Globe' was introduced in 1989 and should be sought out by those raising artichokes in warmer climates like California. Large-scale commercial growers prefer vegetatively propagated stock, as these are essentially clonal, which ensures uniformity, and many growers periodically edit their fields by eliminating under-performing older strains while propagating more vigorous selected clones.

The seed-raised stock, while quicker to market, is less consistent, with more diversity occurring in the field. But savvy consumers seem to enjoy multi-colored buds and the ease of growing an organic product without the worry of pathogens often passed on in vegetatively propagated stock.

RAISING FROM SEED

Artichoke seed, if procured from a reputable seed house, shouldn't need pre-chilling, as fresh seed will germinate quickly. Reputable seed suppliers test their seed (or store their artichoke seeds cold). Always check the growing guide for artichokes (available on most seed company websites) to see if they suggest pre-chilling.

Seeds need to be started early, at least 8 to 10 weeks before your frost-free date—you'll need time to set young transplants outdoors to properly vernalize the seedlings when temperatures are still below 55°F, which may be the trickiest part of the entire process.

It is helpful to use the right containers with artichoke seedlings, as large and robust transplants perform best in the garden. Deep root-training types of cell containers are ideal, as artichokes are tap-rooted. The deeper the pot, the better—this will prevent roots encircling at the bottom of the pot.

If you can't find root trainers, 4- to 6-inch-deep containers will suffice. I prefer to sow in larger containers to avoid damaging roots, which appreciate room to spread without competition. Take care when using plug trays—be sure to choose deep cells and transplant plugs as soon as leaves appear to avoid any root disturbance.

Soil is always a controversial matter, but soilless mix is safest to avoid pathogens. I use a commercial-grade sterile soil mix called Pro-Mix BX (it's what the big growers use), and I have never found an acceptable substitute at retail. If you prefer to use a peat-free mix, a homemade mix comprised of ⅓ compost, ⅓ garden loam, and ⅓ perlite will do.

Germination temperature can be confusing if you are looking for information online. While it is true that artichokes like bottom heat and warmer soil in which to germinate, they are rather specific about how hot they want it. Failure often occurs when a heating mat is set too warm, as that can delay germination just as much as cold soil can.

TOP: Purple Sicilian or 'Purple of Romagna'. **BOTTOM LEFT:** 'Violetta di Chioggia'. **BOTTOM RIGHT:** 'Gros Vert de Laon', an heirloom French variety.

The ideal range for daytime temperatures during germination is between 70°F and 80°F. Sow seed ¼-inch deep and cover. A soil and air thermometer is helpful for growing artichokes. As soon as seedlings emerge, adjust the temperature to be slightly cooler (60°F to 70°F) to help seedlings grow sturdier. A temperature shift to even cooler at night helps many plants, but particularly artichokes. A slight drop to 55°F to 60°F will stimulate healthier growth. Since you will most likely be using an artificial lighting system, this temperature shift will occur naturally as lights turn on and off. Use a timer and set it for 16 hours of daylight and 8 hours of darkness. This should work for most other vegetable seedlings as well.

Artichokes appreciate high fertility, and a healthy seedling is more likely to be resistant to insects and disease. Artichokes are one crop with which I am not afraid to use a chemical-based, water-soluble fertilizer (the blue kind), but one with a balanced analysis. If you prefer to use only organic fertilizer, be sure to look for a balanced feed (not just seaweed or fish emulsion). You'll need one that the plants can access quickly, rather than a slow-release variety.

Any pest concerns indoors should be limited, but expect aphids if you are raising plants under lights. Fungus gnats can become a problem when using fertilizer. A good regimen of allowing the soil to dry almost completely between waterings will help.

HOW TO VERNALIZE PLANTS

Vernalization sounds more complicated than it actually is. It's just a metabolic process that stimulates, in this case, a perennial plant to switch from a vegetative stage to a reproductive stage. This means simply that when exposed to a brief cold period, artichoke plants will be induced to form flower buds.

What we are attempting here is to trick the young plants into believing that they've survived a "mini winter." A Mediterranean winter is typically cool and wet. Vernalization can be accomplished quickly, in just 7 to 10 days after exposing the plants to a few days of temperatures between 34°F and 55°F. The process works best on young plants that have produced at least seven or eight leaves.

In the northeastern United States, where I live, I simply set my plants outdoors for a week or so sometime before May 10th, when they are most likely to experience a period of cooler weather. It can be a bit tricky, as weather is unpredictable, so keep an eye on the forecast and use your knowledge about the weather in your area.

Studies have recently shown that this treatment works with many varieties of artichokes, but it works best with those bred for annual production, with 'Imperial Star' and 'Northern Star' performing the best, even better than 'Green Globe Improved' outside of California.

Seedlings can handle a light frost, especially once set in the ground, but keep protection (such as floating row covers) nearby for the first few weeks as globe artichoke seedlings are susceptible to hard frosts. While a hard frost won't kill a plant, it will damage flower stalks if they are forming.

TRANSPLANTING OUTSIDE

Seedlings can be set out in the open garden early if threats of hard freezes have passed— ideally this occurs immediately after the seedlings have been vernalized. Globe artichokes prefer fertile soil. Before transplanting, prepare beds with additional granular plant food (20-20-20), or well-rotted manure and compost if you are growing organic. These organic amendments are best applied in the previous autumn, especially if you are using blood meal, bone meal, kelp, or other slow-release fertilizers.

MULCH AND WATER

Black plastic is the preferred mulch both for commercial growers and for home growers. It provides benefits such as warming the soil and preserving moisture, not to mention weed suppression. It works best for me as organic mulches encourage infestations of the highly invasive Asian jumping worm (*Amynthas agrestis*). A drip irrigation system applied under the mulch is also helpful.

FERTILITY REQUIREMENTS OUTSIDE

Globe artichokes are heavy feeders. A high-nitrogen formula is recommended at planting time, but later use one that is more evenly balanced, such as a 10-10-10 or a 20-20-20.

Most university studies advise rich, fertile soil. Conventional fertilizer should be applied as a granular sidedressing before the black plastic mulch is laid down. Organic feed includes rotted manures and balanced granular sources.

CULTURE IN MILD CLIMATES

Propagation for most home gardeners in cold climates is from seed, but in California, the United Kingdom, and near the Mediterranean, vegetative propagation by division is the preferred method especially with older and heirloom perennial varieties. As there are many named selections that are regional or protected, this remains the only way to obtain a genetically pure variety that may produce deep violet buds or long, pointed forms.

Treatment is similar to other perennial crops such as rhubarb. Root divisions should be taken from healthy plants in March or April, ideally from those with two or more shoots. Alternatively, in mild-winter areas, nursery-grown perennial container plants are often available. Perennial selections should be divided every 2 or 3 years to maintain vitality, and the soil amended to retain vigor. Plants can become very long-lived.

WHY GROW YOUR OWN?

With all this criticism, you may be wondering why anyone would bother to grow artichokes at all. But I think it goes without saying that if you love artichokes, no argument needs to be made. If you are thinking about trying them,

'Chianti'.

I offer this encouragement: globe artichokes are not only fun to grow, they make beautiful plants in the garden even if you don't pick the buds—handsome specimen plants that will trigger comments from anyone who visits, and unpicked buds will bloom. Most importantly, I cannot overemphasize that a home-raised artichoke is superior to anything you could buy at a market, and potentially could convert even the most sophomoric of eaters. They are indeed the "lobster of the vegetable kingdom."

VARIETIES

'Imperial Star'	'Sienna'	'Carciofo Romanesco'
'Violetta de Chioggia'	'Chianti'	'Violetta Precoce'
'Colorado Star'	'Fiesole'	'Albenga Purple'
'Grande Buerre'	'King'	'Brindisi'
'Green Globe'	'Vert de Laon' or 'Vert de Leon'	'Paestum'
'Green Globe Improved' (introduced 1989)	'Explorer'	'Roman'
'Purple Sicilian'	'Apollo'	
'Big Heart'	'Baby Anzio'	

CABBAGE, KALE, BROCCOLI, AND CAULIFLOWER

While the brassicas are a fairly diverse family in terms of general appearance (ranging from rutabagas to dinosaur kale), there is a good deal of similarity in their culture. First off, all brassicas are heavy feeders and respond well to soils rich in organic matter with plenty of aged manure or compost.

All brassicas are best grown from seed. It may seem wasteful because you will probably only need a few seeds from an entire package, but there is no way around it. If you don't start your own seed you may be limited at the nursery where the only variety you may find is one labeled cabbage. The most common mistake home gardeners make when it comes to brassicas is buying plants too early in spring. Another common mistake is starting seeds too early at home, either indoors or outdoors. It's common to think of cabbage as a cold-weather crop but new research shows us that cabbage can avoid many of the insect perils that have plagued it and other brassica crops if seeds are sown a bit later.

Brassicas must be rotated in the garden from year to year to keep down any brassica pathogens that are soilborne. Rotate every other year if your main threat is the cabbage root maggot. Cabbage root maggots and other pests are major issues for almost all brassicas and are difficult to eradicate without insecticides, but there are new methods for how to outsmart them. The best practices for avoiding outbreaks are good soil management, cleaning up debris from previous brassica crops, and crop rotation. See the section on cabbage for specific steps regarding pest control.

CABBAGE

Brassica oleracea var. *capitata*

It shouldn't be surprising to anyone that cabbage is considered a very old vegetable. Its origin dates back to at least 600 BC, when it was first selected from a wild brassica species. A sturdy vegetable with the ability to feed many, it was indispensable through famines, plagues, war-times, harsh winters, and other times of extreme poverty and hardship. As such, some cultures are loath to associate any positive attributes to the cabbage. Its less-than-romantic scent probably plays a part in that too (let's face it—overcooked cabbage can be stinky). Add to its proletarian image and its smell the fact that cabbage is relatively difficult to grow for home gardeners, and it's amazing that the cabbage has lasted with us this long, let alone thrived. Still, more than 75 million tons of cabbage are grown worldwide every year, even though only a small fraction of that amount comes from home gardens.

CHOOSING A VARIETY

Cabbage is divided into three groups based on season length and days to maturity: early, midseason, and late. All three categories offer unique and flavorful characteristics making them suitable for distinct uses in the kitchen.

OPPOSITE: 'Storage No. 4' is a late-season storage cabbage developed by plant breeder Don Reed of Cortland, New York. It was selected for having a solid, crisp head and exceptionally delicious flavor with the ability to hold these qualities in cold storage until spring.

Early cabbage. This cabbage is super-tender and sweet, with a texture so crisp and fresh that it can be used like iceberg lettuce, which it resembles. Because it has less sulfur, it's a good choice if you find winter-storage cabbage to be too strong of a flavor. It's best uncooked and used in salads, slaws, and similar raw dishes. The best early cabbage grows in a long, cool spring with uninterrupted access to moisture and nutrients.

Midseason and late cabbage. Also called green cabbages, these form firmer heads and store better than early cabbage. Late cabbage in particular is a true storage cabbage that is pure white inside and extremely dense. These are ideal choices for sauerkraut, pickling, and any braised dish. Late cabbage is good for coleslaw, but it will depend on the variety, as some are too dense or fibrous. Flathead types are often preferred for their tenderness. With improved storage techniques, many varieties of green midseason cabbage are now treated as storage cabbage, shipped from the Southern Hemisphere during the off-season and appearing in markets year-round. You can distinguish green cabbage from true storage cabbage by the hard, white density of the latter.

MASTERING CABBAGE

The cultural needs of cabbage are the same as for the other brassicas: rich soil, plenty of water, and protection from insects. Cabbage is a heavy feeder,

BEHIND THE SCENES

Being able to choose varieties that taste and perform better is perhaps the greatest advantage that the home vegetable gardener has. But with cabbages, try to avoid buying commercially raised seedlings. It's not that old varieties are all bad, it's just that with cabbage you are dependent on what the plug grower had access to, which often are short-listed common (read inexpensive) varieties offered by the big seed companies. Many growers and sellers don't really care or know about choice cabbage varieties. They just know that 'Golden Acre' or 'Savoy King' has sold consistently well for 40 years, so why change? Choosing your own varieties from the best seed companies in the world will always be the best option—and the good news is that there are many incredible cabbages to choose from.

INSECTS LOVE CABBAGE

Cabbage and other brassicas are prone to so many pests that many a home gardener has simply given up on them. Major culprits are the larvae of the white cabbage butterfly and cabbage moth you often see fluttering around the garden throughout spring, summer, and fall. The larvae are almost invisible, the only signs of them being holes in the leaves and the dreaded dead ones in the bottom of a bowl or pot. The best and healthiest way to control their damage is by covering the crop for the entire season with a floating row cover. This means blanketing the entire bed—draping the material over wire hoops and pinning it down to the ground, creating an airtight barrier from these little flittering lepidopterans (they will lay their eggs even if plants are left uncovered for just a half day).

Covering the ground with black plastic mulch, when combined with the use of floating row covers, will tuck your cabbage plants into a cocoon of safety. The cover can be removed later in the season as the plants near maturity, but only if you're brave and want to enjoy the beauty of the well-formed heads. This is what I do, as the few larvae that do form seem to focus on the outer leaves and rarely burrow deep inside. An hour-long soak in a sink filled with salted water will take care of any random stragglers.

Methods for combatting the cabbage root maggot have evolved in recent years. Most organic methods are deployed at the time we sow our seeds and when we plant the seedlings. The trick is timing your plantings after the first big hatch of root maggot flies in the spring. It is also important to pay attention to the timing of the other three hatches, as it is the larvae that damage your plants; the flying insects are relatively harmless.

You can reduce the risk of cutworms by rototilling a bed or using a handheld tiller. This will disturb the soil and kill most cutworms by destroying pathways and their environment. While rototilling has been getting a bad rap lately, for large gardens it is still an essential and practical way to till the soil. No one wants to hand-dig a ¼-acre bed with a fork, and soil tillage is important when digging-in compost, manure, or fertilizer. It also reduces weeds, allowing the soil to warm more quickly in the spring.

SEEDBORNE PATHOGENS

Preventing disease in cabbage begins with seed selection, as the surface of cabbage seed is a notorious carrier of a number of dangerous pathogens. Commercial growers treat their seed with something called the hot water method. But for home growers, simply look for seed companies who treat their seeds with heat. Another strategy you can use to avoid disease is to grow varieties that are more resistant. Most F1 hybrids will list their disease resistance in their seed descriptions. With heirlooms, vigor varies, but some old varieties that are open-pollinated are very disease-resistant. If you have concerns, remember that organic F1 hybrids are now offered.

OPPOSITE: 'Caraflex' F1 is a super flavorful, sweet, and crispy cone-shaped early cabbage that can be harvested before July.

NAPA CABBAGE

Brassica rapa subsp. *pekinensis*

Napa cabbage (also called Chinese cabbage) is becoming more popular as a salad vegetable, but its garden culture has rarely been reviewed. To clear up some botany from the very beginning, napa cabbage really shouldn't be considered a true cabbage, as it belongs to the same species of Brassica as the turnip—*Brassica rapa*. This particular subspecies—*pekinensis*—is much more cabbagelike than any other *Brassica rapa* though. Most people assume that it is a cabbage, as it forms a head and is often sold alongside cabbage at the market.

A quick-growing crop, napa cabbage is surprisingly easy to grow, although it is best grown in the fall rather than in the spring. Early summer crops can be successful, though, as long as you set plants out after the soil and nighttime temperature warm to above 50°F for a few days.

Seeds can be sown in cell containers in late August when the weather is still warm, as seeds require temperatures of 75°F to 85°F to germinate. Seeds germinate within a few days and young plants grow fast. Seedlings like it a bit cooler once they start growing though, with air temperatures between 60°F and 75°F being ideal. In many climates, this typically happens naturally in September, which makes napa culture rather foolproof.

Seedlings should be set into a prepared bed when their third or fourth leaves begin to open. Spacing depends on the variety—12 inches apart for miniature-sized varieties, or 18 to 24 inches apart for full-sized ones. Water seedlings in with a 10-10-10 water-soluble fertilizer and cover the entire bed with a floating row cover to discourage cabbage butterflies and cabbage moths.

Napa cabbage grows optimally with plenty of water, appreciating the gradually shortening daylengths of autumn, and growing in soil that has high fertility and additional organic matter like aged manure or compost. It makes an excellent crop for secondary plantings when the tomatoes or beans are through for the summer, and can extend a garden well into fall. Colder nights in fall won't cause plants to bolt, as the nights are getting longer.

VARIETIES

'Rubicon' F1 hybrid (52 days)—A full-sized napa cabbage that is slow to bolt and tolerant to black speck.

'Minuet' F1 hybrid (48 days)—Miniature variety that is quick-growing, forming dense 10-inch heads tolerant to black speck. Good for raised beds and smaller gardens as you can arrange a matrix of plants spaced 12 inches apart.

'Red Dragon' F1 hybrid (60 days)—A beautiful new variety with purple-red leaves that forms slightly looser heads of a very fine quality. Can be raised through the summer in very cold climates, but best as a fall crop elsewhere.

OPPOSITE: 'Minuet' F1 is a hybrid mini-napa cabbage that is perfect for fall crops in raised beds or containers.

KALE

Even though kale was said to be enjoyed by the early Romans, it's hard to imagine anyone really "enjoying" kale until the late twentieth century. It was a common vegetable in colonial gardens, but usually as a last-choice winter green due to its sturdiness. It was more likely to be used in long-cooking soups and later as a garnish in salad bars in the 1970s. In fact, few old recipes exist for kale other than its use in Portuguese soups or as "poor man's spinach."

Nineteenth-century gardening texts, even in France where kale was grown often, comment that the plant is hardy but "more curious than useful," which says a lot. In early America, it was often referred to as borecole. The various rough-textured brassicas were often grouped along with what we know today as Russian or Siberian kale, and with collards and crops more fit as fodder than as fine table fare.

Today, kale is almost an entirely different product. Eating raw kale is a surprisingly recent trend, taking off with the advent of food knowledge and the health benefits attributed to many greens. A nineteenth-century farmer would be shocked to see kale served raw in salads, roasted in wood-fired ovens, or even toasted into kale chips.

Gardeners have embraced the newly redefined kale and adopted even better varieties virtually unknown outside of Italy just 40 years ago. Now you can find greenhouse-grown baby kale picked at the young leaf stage like spinach, and many types of interesting heirloom varieties like 'Lacinato'—the Tuscan "black cabbage" so dark and flavorful and more tender than traditional curly kales. Russian kale, with its tender, lobed leaves—some as colorful as the ornamental kales found in autumnal displays—is also gaining popularity.

How you choose the varieties you want should begin with how you plan to use them. It makes sense to grow more than one variety when planning a garden, as different varieties have different uses. A Tuscan flat-leaf type like dinosaur kale is great for fall and winter use in raw salads and as baby kale, while Portuguese kale is ideal for soups and stews. Both the Tuscan black and the curly kales are best for cooking—they roast well and are great for making kale chips or serving with autumn root vegetables. Russian kales, however, are far too tender for the roasting oven, and are more fit for raw consumption. Talented chefs are making all sorts of dishes with kale today, from kale "butter" pureed with chickpeas or white beans to kale pesto for pasta. If you are processing kale, go for the darkest varieties for the most dramatic color and impact—the Lacinato types are best as they are less fibrous than curly kale.

Baby kale is challenging in the home garden as it is a crop designed for hoop house culture. You need at least a quarter pound of seed for a small bed that will only produce enough to fill a large bowl.

ABOVE: Baby kale is just immature kale seedlings and can be raised as a spring or fall crop from transplants, but long-season kale is best if grown from seedlings that were planted later and never exposed to cold spring temperatures. The same goes for the more tender Red Russian kale and Tuscan kale. **BELOW AND OPPOSITE:** 'Black Magic', a variety of Tuscan kale.

Unlike its brassica kin, kale can be considered a four-season crop, but plants sown in spring will never perform as well as a long-season crop—stems will become too woody and yields will diminish through the summer. Grow early kale as a young or baby green, and save the main-harvest for long-season kale set out into the garden in early summer. A third crop of kale can be sown in autumn for culture in cold frames or mini-hoop houses through the winter, depending on the severity of your climate.

Main season kale grows best when seed is sown near the summer solstice outdoors. Pots 3 inches in diameter are best to reduce root disturbance. Seeds will germinate best at warmer temperatures (75°F), often emerging in just 5 days in summer. Once seedlings emerge, grow the young plants until they form their first true set of leaves. At this time plants can be set out into the garden to mature by mid- to late summer.

Sowing seed directly outdoors in individual cell containers or 3-inch pots remains the best way to ensure the healthiest seedlings. Seed sown outside benefits from a slightly later sowing though, with mid-May to mid-June being the ideal time for USDA Zones 6 and lower. Seedlings raised indoors can be transplanted with minimal root disturbance once the weather warms. Be sure to harden plants off first with a week or two outdoors in a protected area.

Space plants 24 to 30 inches apart in the garden. Prepare the soil as for all brassicas by tilling to help reduce cutworms and aid in hilling the bed so you can quickly cover it with a plastic or synthetic mulch. Black plastic is preferred—it will significantly reduce the need for weeding and watering, and will also help retain nitrogen levels.

The most exceptional results will come from using nonorganic fertilizer, though, as the blend of ammonium nitrate and ammonium sulfate, along with the triple superphosphate and potassium chloride, will help balance out the specific needs. A good option is to use both organic and nonorganic feed—the nonorganic product is short-lived (leaching out in a matter of weeks), while the organic is released more slowly. The organic feed also has micronutrients, which can be helpful.

'Redbor' kale in the late-summer garden can offer harvests through a mild winter, even one with snow.

While few gardeners worry about soil pH during the growing season, a test in spring and one during the summer are helpful, especially if you are applying organic fertilizers—they have sources of nitrogen that are either negatively or positively charged. Fish emulsion is good for kale because it is more alkaline. Kale absorbs nutrients best with a soil pH of 6.5 to 7.5, similar to cabbage. Avoid bat guano as it is too acidic and will cause low pH problems.

INSECT AND PEST CONTROL

Kale is highly vulnerable to insect damage, and there is no organic way to control an infestation of cabbage moth or cabbage butterfly larvae other than using a floating row cover. Next to kohlrabi, though, kale seems to be less plagued in some years from the larvae. But if a worm in the kale salad is a concern, cover the crop with a tight tent of floating row cover fabric from the moment you plant it (see page 58).

VARIETIES

The Russian kales are beautiful tall plants with flat leaves. They look rather unlike any other kale and are rarely seen in markets because of their tendency to wilt once picked.

'Red Russian' (60 days)—Gray-green leaves with reddish veins. Best grown as a fall crop as the optimum temperature range is between 60°F and 70°F. Sow 3 months before the first frost to ensure a harvest of mature leaves. It can be raised as a winter crop in mild areas where temperatures rarely drop below 32°F.

LACINATO, DINOSAUR, OR TUSCAN BLACK KALES

'Toscano'—Italian heirloom variety with very savoyed or blistered leaves so distinctive with these varieties. Like all Tuscan heirloom-type kale, sow later for longer fall crops (May or June planting).

'Black Magic'—A choice selection, this improved Toscano type has long leaves that are narrower.

STANDARD CURLY KALE

'Winterbor' (55 days)—The common curly green kale, but a hybrid typically with excellent uniformity and a long harvest season.

'Redbor' (55 days)—The standard red-leaved curly kale. Attractive and useful all the way around—both as a garnish or in flower arrangements—throughout the summer, fall, and winter. Harvest stems from the bottom up and grow it as a cut-and-come-again vegetable.

'Starbor' (55 days)—A faster-maturing variety with stems that are more tender. Short internodes (the space between the leaves) give the plant a bushier appearance and more kale leaves for the kitchen. It's a good spring-maturing kale.

'Darkibor' (75 days)—A curly kale a bit less curly than others. Popular as baby kale.

PORTUGUESE KALE

'Beira' F1 hybrid (80 days)—A massive and glorious plant, it grows best if spaced wider than other kales. Sow seed in mid-May and set plants out anytime between June and early July, spacing them 36 inches apart to allow the large leaves to form. Will produce well into winter. This choice and hard-to-find kale is commonly used in Portuguese dishes, particularly soups.

While some growers use *Bacillus thuringiensis* (Bt), a few growers are concerned about its safety as a product. I prefer natural solutions, such as harvesting kale after a hard frost has killed every creature. Or I use a vast stretch of floating row cover set over wire hoops, conveniently available now from a few online sources and seed suppliers.

Tent the entire bed with the floating row cover (order it early so that you have it ready at planting time). Waiting until you see insect damage is usually too late, as egg cases are tricky to find, and cabbage butterflies and moths emerge early. To make things more challenging, their larvae are almost invisible on plants because they are tiny and green.

BROCCOLI
Brassica oleracea

In North America, broccoli is a rather recent introduction, having arrived with the first waves of Italian immigrants in the late nineteenth century. Many gardeners assume that broccoli shares the same culture as cauliflower and cabbage, so they treat these crops in similar ways. Although the seed catalog may state that broccoli prefers cool weather, that doesn't mean it actually likes cool weather—it really means that broccoli can stand cool weather when mature. Nevertheless, it demands heat to germinate well—near 85°F, to be precise.

Most brassicas evolved from the same wild plant, and broccoli shares many of the same needs as its brassica brethren: long, cool growing seasons, consistent watering, and soil rich in organic matter. It also is plagued by the same pests, especially the larvae of cabbage butterflies and moths, which can devour a plant in just a few days.

TYPES OF BROCCOLI

The most familiar type is the typical green broccoli sometimes referred to as Calabrese or Calabrese-type broccoli, depending on what country you live in. In England, green heading broccoli is usually called simply "Calabrese," while in the rest of the world Calabrese is a type of broccoli with many varietal names. In addition to the familiar Calabrese broccoli, you can find many varieties of standard green broccoli. Some have smaller heads, while others form large heads in the autumn. A few varieties are better at producing side branches for a second crop, while some are best as a single harvest, producing a massive head.

RAISING BROCCOLI FROM SEED

Broccoli is best raised from seed sown in early summer or midsummer and planted as a fall crop. Early crops can be had in the spring in cool climates if sown early, but few recommend starting seeds indoors given the high likelihood of incurring insect damage in the spring. The best results come from broccoli seedlings that are started at home, outdoors in cell containers. Timing is key, as seed sown in late spring until right around the summer solstice will grow into the finest quality broccoli. Seedlings raised in this manner will yield flavorful, abundant crops from mid-September through late autumn.

Sow two or three seeds into a washed and sterilized cell pack. Use sterile soilless mix, and set the seeds into each hole at a ¼-inch depth. In June or early July, seeds will germinate quickly, often in 4 or 5 days. Monitor soil moisture, especially if containers are in full sun, as plants can dry out and wilt in a single day, which can stunt them permanently.

OPPOSITE: 'Imperial' F1 broccoli is a strong grower, particularly for late-summer crops.

CAULIFLOWER

Experienced gardeners know that producing good harvests of cauliflower in a home garden is challenging. But like most brassica crops, the flavor of fresh cauliflower is exceptional and rarely experienced by most people unless they keep a vegetable garden.

As with all brassicas, success with cauliflower comes from taking the time to provide the plants with precisely what they need (rich soil, consistent moisture, and protection from damaging insect larvae). Wisely timing the crop is also extremely important.

The easiest way to achieve this is to forego buying seedlings in the spring at nurseries—they are often sold too early and are too large for setting out into the garden. Even if a seedling appears healthy at a garden center, the time you should set it out in the garden is probably incorrect—especially if you want to avoid the mid-May hatch of cabbage root maggots.

Cauliflower is best grown as a late-summer and fall crop—it prefers the warmer summer months to aid germination and growth. As an adult plant, it reacts best to decreasing day lengths and will form larger heads as nights get longer. Autumn weather won't harm it, as it

OPPOSITE: While commonly known as cheddar cauliflower, most orange varieties are named hybrids. 'Flame Star' is one of the finest, with large curds and the largest heads coming from crops that were planted out as late as mid-August.

can handle even heavy frosts with little harm. If attempting an early summer crop, start seeds 6 weeks early indoors. Seed prefers to be warm, germinating best in soils near 85°F. Immediately after seeds emerge, the containers should be moved to a cooler location, but still bright. If starting seeds outdoors for a late summer or autumn crop, start them directly in the sun, or on a porch or deck where they can grow for a few weeks in temperatures between 50°F and 70°F. This will make them strong and sturdy.

Seedlings should be set out into the garden by mid-June in colder areas, but in warmer areas set them out later. The larger-heading cauliflower varieties require longer growing seasons and have environmental triggers that stimulate head formation in the autumn—mainly longer nights and gradually lowering temperatures. Earlier or midseason varieties that form smaller heads (80- to 90-day varieties) can mature in mid- to late summer.

All cauliflower is best sown between mid-June and mid-July in pots set outside. Kept well-watered and fertilized, cauliflower responds beautifully—any reduction in food will affect the quality of the crop. These are not plants you can ever grow lean.

WHAT WENT WRONG

Selecting the right moment to harvest cauliflower is very important for your crop. If you wait too long, the cauliflower heads will "rice," which means the heads will start to open up and then bolt. Ricing is often caused by planting too early, so pay careful attention to the days to maturity listed for your variety. Simply work backward from the first frost date and subtract the days to maturity for the plant. And if warm weather threatens, harvest cauliflower heads early to avoid over-matured heads. Heads that "rice" however are still okay to eat. In fact, in some Chinese provinces this is the preferred way to harvest cauliflower.

RAISING A FALL CROP

Although you can do spring plantings, cauliflower will always grow best when raised as a fall crop. Like most brassicas, they are biennial, and the gradual introduction of cool weather more naturally suits their growth habits. The methods are similar to those suggested for growing brussels sprouts or broccoli, and often the finest crops will come from seed sown in early to mid-summer. Late-maturing cauliflower forms tighter and often larger heads, and is significantly sweeter and more flavorful than early cauliflower. Cauliflower grown commercially is always grown as a fall crop.

Cauliflower makes a great winter crop wherever winters are mild. Where summers are particularly cool, you may need to adjust dates accordingly. In Arizona or Southern California, excellent crops can be planted as late as mid-October, while in Atlantic Canada or northern Vermont, May 30 might be more appropriate.

PESTS AND PROBLEMS

Like most brassicas, cauliflower is prone to many diseases and insects. Start by choosing the best disease-resistant seed you can buy. Ask if it was tested for black rot, as that is often spread via seed, especially seed from value sources or questionable distributors. The most annoying pests with any brassica are cabbage moths and cabbage butterflies. The cabbage moth (*Mamestra brassicae*) is an unremarkable speckled brown, and the cabbage looper (*Trichoplusia ni*) looks equally nondescript, but most gardeners will recognize the third pest, the white cabbage butterfly (*Pieris brassicae*). This small white butterfly is commonly seen fluttering around gardens all summer long. The best way to control larva damage is by covering the plants with a floating row cover.

LEFT: Young cauliflower seedlings that were raised using old cell containers make the strongest plants. **ABOVE:** A floating row cover can serve many purposes when it comes to brassica crops. Not only can it create a warmer microclimate to extend the growing season in early spring and in the late autumn, but it can also help alleviate insect problems throughout the growing season, particularly by controlling cabbage butterfly larvae. **OPPOSITE:** 'Veronica' F1, a new Romanesco-type cauliflower.

VARIETIES

Cauliflower varieties can be grouped by type ranging from their shape and form to their color and season. Botanically more complex varieties can be grouped as annuals as well as biennials, and some grouped as Asian. There are self-blanching varieties, which are good for tropical climates.

TRADITIONAL VARIETIES

'Skywalker' F1 hybrid (80 days)—Premium late-season variety with large, self-wrapping heads. Best only as a fall crop.

'Snow Crown' F1 hybrid (50 days)—The standard white midseason and medium-sized cauliflower. Prone to moisture stress and heat stress, which can cause it to blush purple. Can handle light frosts in the fall. AAS winner.

COLORED TYPE

'Graffiti' F1 hybrid (80 days)—The standard purple cauliflower, best raised as a late summer- and fall-maturing crop. Beautiful dark-violet heads.

'Flame Star' F1 hybrid (62 days)—A pale-orange cauliflower that is more tolerant of heat and stress; great for midsummer and fall crops.

'Cheddar' F1 hybrid (58 days)—The premium orange-curd variety that is so popular at farmers' markets as a specialty crop. Can be raised as a summer-maturing harvest or in the fall for larger heads.

'Vitaverde' F1 hybrid (71 days)—A true all-green cauliflower (that is not Romanesco-type). Good tolerance as a summer crop.

ROMANESCO-TYPE (BROCCOFLOWER)

'Veronica' F1 hybrid (78 days)—A newer Romanesco-type with trademark fractal-shaped points and a long-season maturing habit. Best as a fall crop.

KOHLRABI

Kohlrabi is a subvariety of the family Brassicaceae. Botanically it is blessed with a mouthful of a Latin name—*Brassica oleracea* var. *gongylodes*—yet it is a far humbler crop than its exotic name and looks imply. Kohlrabi looks like no other member of the cabbage family. You could say that it is just a type of cabbage that developed with a swollen stem, but that would be oversimplifying things.

I am not ashamed to admit that kohlrabi is my favorite vegetable. This preference is shared by many who enjoy the mild flavor similar to the inner stem of broccoli or cabbage, but sweeter. Many believe it to be a kind of turnip, but it isn't. It tastes like the sweetest cousin to its relative the cabbage, but kohlrabi is neither a turnip nor a cabbage, and certainly not a turnip-cabbage. When kohlrabi appear at the market in autumn and winter, many forgo trying them because they look a little creepy, with an appearance that causes prop stylists to use them as the perfect food prop for aliens to eat in science fiction films.

In the home garden, it's a quick-growing crop that can be sown early indoors (it germinates best in warmth around 80°F) but then relocated outside as the weather warms. One of the few brassicas that do well when started early under lights, its maturation rate allows you to grow multiple kohlrabi harvests throughout the year.

As soon as the threat of hard frost is over, transplant kohlrabi seedlings that have been hardened off outdoors for a week. Cabbage root maggots are rarely a problem, and cabbage butterflies seem hardly to bother with them (if they do, they focus on the leaves and not the stem). A winter crop in warm climates and a summer crop in cold climates, kohlrabi is flexible and tolerant of extremes. Best of all, it's an economical crop—it can be set out into the garden in a grid with plants spaced at 8 to 10 inches, offering a big harvest from a relatively small area. A common complaint about kohlrabi is that it all seems to mature at the same time, which isn't a problem for some, yet it's worth noting if you want a continuous supply through the summer. Sowing seed at 3-week intervals in smaller amounts might be needed.

Kohlrabi varieties are available in both purple and "white" types or light green varieties. They look and taste the same once peeled, but older and heirloom white selections such as 'Kossak' are your best choices if you want larger kohlrabi that does not become woody. The greatest problem you may encounter is bulbs that split if they have been kept in the garden too long and are exposed to heavy rain after a dry period.

OPPOSITE: Kohlrabi should be picked young, just as the bulbs reach the size of chicken eggs or tennis balls. Most varieties can split if allowed to get any larger.

Knowing when to pick kohlrabi is important. The best advice is to pick sooner rather than later, around the time when the spherical stem reaches the size of a tennis ball.

Harvest the bulbs by pulling the entire plant out of the ground and cutting the root end. Peeled and either boiled or steamed, then served with butter and salt is a favored method for consuming kohlrabi. Like most summer delicacies such as sweet corn or spring turnips, the flavor of fresh kohlrabi doesn't need much improvement.

VARIETIES

'Quickstar' F1 hybrid (37 days)—A very early green selection that will mature in just a month's time—perfect for early spring and fall crops.

'Kolibri' F1 hybrid (45 days)—The darkest purple variety, very choice with a white, crispy interior.

'Azure Star' open-pollinated (48 days)—A purple open-pollinated variety that should be harvested while the bulbs are small (2 to 3 inches in diameter).

'Kossak' F1 hybrid (80 days)—A massive, long-season variety from eastern Europe (where kohlrabi is popular). Bulbs can grow to 8 inches in diameter.

TOP: Set out early, kohlrabi grows quickly in the spring and can be harvested in just a month and a half. **ABOVE:** Young kohlrabi 'Kolibri' seedlings are already hinting at their bright purple color. **OPPOSITE:** 'Kossak' is an F1 hybrid kohlrabi that can grow as large as a softball and still be tender and crispy.

TURNIPS AND RUTABAGAS

Turnips arrived on the scene earlier than most other brassicas because they required less selection. The fact that a turnip is primarily a swollen root or swollen stem and not an elaborate floral bud (like cauliflower or broccoli) makes the plant simpler.

Most scholars agree that the origin of turnips dates back further than any written account; some even believe that the turnip helped introduce more meat into our diets by allowing early tribes to domesticate grazing animals by feeding them turnips in winter around the fifteenth century BC—before grains were widely available. The turnip is also credited with saving thousands of lives in times of famine, especially in a pre-potato world so dependent on seasonal harvests of winter storage vegetables. Pliny the Elder famously wrote that it was one of the most important vegetables of his time.

There are plenty of people today who indulge in their sweet and slightly bitter or nutty flavor. Spring and salad turnips are big in Asia, particularly in Japan, where the vegetable is highly regarded. In North America and eastern Europe, it's the rutabaga (or yellow storage turnip) that has remained a seasonal staple. In these cooler climates, many regional varieties are shared and enjoyed through the often long and harsh winters.

Turnips and rutabagas could be considered the "soul food" of cold climates. Their

OPPOSITE: 'Hakurei', Japanese white turnips.

satisfying horseradish flavor is sweetened when mashed with butter, and enhanced when pickled or braised. And no pot roast is complete without the addition of rutabaga.

SPRING (SALAD) TURNIPS

Spring or salad turnips are radishlike in texture and flavor, and nearly as fast-growing. The most common varieties are purple-topped or completely white (Tokyo Cross types), but others are purple, golden, or red-skinned. All are tolerant of light frosts, so these fast-growing vegetables can be sown directly into cold soil in the early spring, once the soil temperatures are above 45°F. As a fall crop, the seed should be sown in late summer, 60 days before the first frost. Like all brassicas, a summer sowing will germinate more readily, given the warmer temperatures. Salad turnips planted in the spring are more plagued by insects than later crops. The use of a floating row cover is essential to keep pests at bay—flea beetles, root maggots, and cabbage moths are common. These turnips—if grown well in organic soil with consistent moisture—will be ready to pick 40 to 50 days after sowing. When sowing, use a seed spacer if possible to carefully set seeds into the soil 1 to 2 inches apart. Thin the seedlings later, rather than transplanting individual plants—turnips and rutabagas do not transplant well. Salad turnips are rarely considered a storage vegetable, but they can be refrigerated for up to a month after picking, or be pickled or preserved.

VARIETIES

ASIAN AND SALAD TURNIPS

'Hakurei' F1 hybrid (38 days)—An improved Japanese salad turnip that is ready to harvest in just one month under ideal conditions (damp, rich soil in full sun).

'Scarlet Queen' F1 hybrid (43 days)—A red-skinned white turnip that matures quickly and looks like a red beet until you cut into the crisp, white flesh. Best as a fall crop, but can be grown where springtime weather is cool.

'Purple Top' open-pollinated (50 days)—The classic turnip in America (particularly as a winter crop in warm climates and as a spring and fall crop in cold climates).

RUTABAGA VARIETIES

Rutabaga or yellow turnips are great for winter storage and are strictly a fall crop.

'Helenor' open-pollinated (90 days)—A purple-topped variety with yellow flesh. Very uniform, with high sugar content and long storage ability.

'Laurentian' open-pollinated (95 days)—Long-season yellow-flesh variety best sown just after the summer solstice and harvested after a light frost. A classic purple-top yellow storage rutabaga that forms uniform yet slightly smaller roots.

WHITE TURNIP VARIETIES

'Gilfeather' open-pollinated heirloom (90 days)—A classic white-fleshed, green-topped heirloom. Less fibrous and very choice. Hard to find in markets except in cooler climates.

'Macomber' heirloom (95 days)—A regional historical variety from Westport, Massachusetts, that dates back to the seventeenth century in America. Highly prized by chefs. Similar to 'Gilfeather'. Seeds are available rarely, often from Landreth Seeds.

LEFT: Rutabaga 'Laurentian'. **OPPOSITE:** 'Scarlet Queen' is a crispy white turnip with a bright red skin not unlike a radish.

RADISHES

Raphanus raphanistrum subsp. *sativus*

The radish has early roots, but was transformed into the vegetable we know today through selection, probably in France with its history of round and long red radishes. There, on farms outside of Paris, it went to vegetable charm school, matriculating as a woody, yellow, turniplike root and graduating as a lovely, red, spherical rootlet. Its improved texture meant that it no longer needed boiling or braising, but was suddenly suitable for eating fresh. The globe radish became immensely popular throughout Europe and in Colonial America. On the other side of the planet, the radish reached China centuries earlier, migrating from Egypt as a yellow, woody root. In China, it evolved along a completely different path, being bred over the centuries into what we now know as the daikon and other long and tender Asian radishes. These are becoming more and more popular. This is why we often see red spring salad radishes listed as French Breakfast types while the long-rooted, white radishes grown in Fall are listed as Japanese or Asian varieties.

OPPOSITE: Salad radishes can be raised with less insect damage at home with a few tweaks, and by ignoring common lore to sow them early. If grown in elevated beds filled with sterile soil later in the spring, you can avoid the brown trails of cabbage root maggots and spots caused by flea beetles.

GROWING RADISHES

All radishes are quick-growing crops that enjoy cool, even cold weather. Sure, radishes can be sown as soon as the soil can be worked, and sure, they will germinate fine in cold soils, but these conditions only invite their most common pest, the cabbage root maggot—the larva of a fly that prefers cold, wet spring soils. This is the larva that causes those brown trails you often see inside a radish (hopefully not after you have bitten into it). Because of their susceptibility to early spring garden pests, commercial radish crops are among the most heavily treated with insecticide. With home-raised crops, you can monitor your radish bed without using chemical treatments.

Radishes can suffer from the same stresses that affect the quality of other brassicas, such as insufficient water, which can cause them to be pithy and hollow, or too much water, which can cause them to split.

In my book, radishes are worth cultivating. Their variety alone will keep the home cook happy, and their colorful shapes and flavors can turn an ordinary crudité plate into a visual celebration.

TYPES OF RADISHES

Radishes can be divided into two main groups: spring/early summer and winter. The spring or early summer radishes are the most familiar to us—they are the small round red and icicle types often sold tied in bunches. The magnificent winter

radishes, however, are becoming more fashionable, with such Instagram stars as the watermelon radish and new purple daikon types. All radishes can today be considered excellent salad vegetables, but they are delicious when cooked as well. The many uses for winter radishes lean towards pickling and preserving, they are often used as sushi, vegetable noodles, and of course, in fresh salads. They can be braised in broths or even preserved or dried in salt.

Black Spanish radishes are appearing in more local markets as well. Once highly valued in the eighteenth and nineteenth centuries—even in North America prior to refrigeration—these strange-looking, slate-black winter storage vegetables still have their fans. Don't be put off by the appearance—they may look like a sphere of charcoal, but inside they are crispy and white, with the flavor of a tender turnip. They can be cooked like turnips or sliced raw into salad. As with any radish, these are best straight from the garden.

With an entirely new world of radishes entering the marketplace, seed catalogs now offer pages of heirloom, hybrid, and even novelty radishes. The rat-tailed radish,

one of my favorites, is grown just for its seedpods. These make great pickles—like skinny okra. Fine as summer fresh snacking while walking through the garden, but they can get quite spicy and hot if the weather becomes warm too quickly.

GROWING SPRING RADISHES

The radish is regarded as the easiest vegetable to grow. If you want to germinate seeds for a kid's science project, radishes offer almost instant gratification. But to grow crispy, white-fleshed radishes outdoors and without insect damage? That's a different story.

The most significant challenge most will face with radishes is overcoming cabbage root maggots (*Delia radicum*)—the destructive white larvae you have seen mentioned with great frequency in this chapter on brassicas. The secret to combatting these pests is to outsmart them. Time your crop to fit somewhere in between the three to five hatches (or flights) that occur throughout the growing season. For a lengthier discussion on how to do this, see the

ABOVE: Young radish seedlings serving a double purpose, identifying a row of onion seedlings. **OPPOSITE TOP LEFT:** 'White Icicle' radishes picked in July. **OPPOSITE TOP RIGHT:** 'Bravo', a purple daikon radish. **OPPOSITE BOTTOM:** Left column, from top to bottom: 'Bravo' F1 daikon, 'Mantanghong' watermelon type, 'Red Meat' watermelon type. Second from the top left: 'Bacchus' F1. Center (vertical white radish): 'Miyashige' daikon. Third column from right, center, horizontal purple radish: 'Bora King' purple daikon. Bottom (horizontal white radish): 'Summer Cross' No. 3 F1.

FROM LEFT TO RIGHT: Rutabaga 'Laurentian', 'Summer White Cross' daikon, 'Nero Tondo' Spanish black radish, 'Hakurei' white turnip, 'Scarlet Queen' red turnip, 'Pusa jamuni' purple daikon, 'Niseko' white turnip. **OPPOSITE:** White 'Niseko' turnips and 'Nero Tondo' Spanish black radish.

section on cabbages, page 55. Smart gardeners know that the time to sow radishes is "just after the first big flight of the root maggots" . . . not as catchy as "as soon as the soil can be worked," but better advice.

MASTERING DAIKON AND OTHER ASIAN RADISHES

It is in the fall that radishes really become exciting. As Western eaters have become more familiar with Asian cuisine, the daikon and other similar radishes are showing up on the covers of food magazines and in trendy food blogs. If you have missed the trend in the West, a trip to Japan will quickly open your eyes to the wonders of the daikon. There, the daikon is treasured and raised with tremendous care. Today, Westerners are finding new uses for the daikon. Chefs grate it into meatballs and dumplings, slice it up for fresh kimchi, or even add it to raw salads. So, if you've never considered growing the daikon radish, now is a great time.

Daikon is a true radish (*Raphanus sativus* var. *longipinnatus*), and its culture is simple enough, similar to the methods shared across all the fall brassicas. Daikon and other Asian radishes are remarkably easy to grow. Try planting them in succession after an early summer crop of beans. Sow the seeds ¾ inch deep from mid-July until August 1st for fall crops in cool climates, and even later in warm climates. Check with your local agricultural university website for accurate planting dates—most list them for all crops.

Spacing is important. Sow seed every 4 to 6 inches as plants will grow large, and quickly. Radishes sown near August 1st can be ready to pick by the end of September, producing roots 2 feet long if all the conditions are right, yet home growers should be happy with any root that reaches 10 inches or more in length. This takes plenty of water, fertilizer, and sunshine. Space rows wide (over 24 inches apart) if you have the room. This will allow you to flood the gutter between rows, or if using plastic mulch, to tuck it in tightly.

Commercial farms often position their Asian radishes in their wettest fields. I plant all my Asian radishes and turnips in early August in a garden near the woods, where it is nearly swampy. Picking fall radishes often requires mudboots but the results are worth the effort.

VARIETIES

'Cherry Belle' open-pollinated (22 days)—Fine quality, standard red globe radish. Early enough for spring crops due to its very short growing season. AAS winner.

'D'Avignon' open-pollinated (21 days)—Perhaps the best for early spring sowing as they are a quick crop that germinates well in cool soils. An improved 'French Breakfast' type—rose-colored, finger-shaped radishes with white tips.

'Easter Egg' open-pollinated (50 days)—Popular colored mix of round radishes. Look for improved strain called 'Easter Egg II'.

'Zlata' heirloom (36 days)—A rare, golden-brown heirloom radish from Poland. An interesting alternative to round red radishes.

ASIAN AND FERMENTING RADISHES

'Green Luobo' open-pollinated (57 days)—A lovely green Asian radish great for fermenting, kimchi, and pickles. Sow in midsummer for fall harvests only, as it will bolt as a spring crop.

'Red Meat' open-pollinated (50 days)—An improved watermelon radish with an unfortunate name. Strictly a summer-sown, fall-harvest radish. Never sow in spring.

'Sweet Baby Daikon' F1 hybrid (44 days)—A beautiful violet short-length daikon suitable for pickles and fermenting as well as fresh use. Strictly a fall crop.

'Miyashige' open-pollinated (50 days)—Fine early daikon. White roots 16 to 18 inches long with green shoulders. The earliest-maturing daikon strictly for summer sowing and fall harvest.

'Summer Cross No. 3' F1 hybrid (55 days)—A premium daikon-type for home growers producing thick roots 16 inches in length. Early to midsummer sowing for late summer to early autumn harvest.

BLACK SPANISH RADISH

'Nero Tondo' open-pollinated (50 days)—A fine strain of black radish that is slow to bolt; it has black skins and white, tender flesh. Can be sown in late spring for summer harvest or midsummer for fall harvest.

COLLARDS

Brassica oleracea var. *acephala*

It's hard to imagine the southern United States without okra and collard greens. Both have an impressive legacy in African-American soul food, but long before collard greens ever entered the cuisine of the Deep South, they were enjoyed as a vegetable throughout much of Europe. In many ways, the collard was known as cabbage before heading forms were selected, and as such is as multinational as any cabbage is today.

Botanically speaking, collards are 100 percent brassicas, belonging to the same subspecies as kale. This should come as no surprise to the gardener—their similarities are rather obvious. Even as recently as the late nineteenth century, kales and collards were often confused and grouped together as "borecole" or "colewort." Both terms were used then for any leafy cabbagelike plants, but mostly for the larger "tree cabbages" that were useful for feeding cattle and horses.

Collards, however, found their audience in southern gardens because they grew well during the winter months (both kale and collards prefer cooler weather). Due to their rugged adaptability, the collard quickly became associated with the diets of poor farmers and slave communities, where many turned to the collard as a substantial, fresh, and available green.

OPPOSITE: 'Champion' collards.

Today collards are enjoyed in much of North America, if not globally, but nowhere are they as essential to the diet as they are in the American South. Along with black-eyed peas and okra, few imported vegetables could ever be considered as all-American as these.

MASTERING TECHNIQUES
TIPS FOR GROWING COLLARDS

- Collards are true southern crops, best grown in the fall or as a winter crop in southern climates.
- Like all brassicas, collards like a soil pH of 7.5, which leans toward alkaline. Lime is required to push pH this high.
- Row covers will help northern growers keep insect larvae away.
- Do not sow seed too early in the spring or start seed indoors.
- Fertilize. Collards want rich soil.
- Most people think collards want heat and humidity, but they prefer cool weather (55°F to 75°F is ideal).

VATES

Vates are collards first introduced in the mid-1940s. VATES is an acronym for the Virginia Truck Experiment Station (now the Hampton Roads Agricultural Research and Extension Center). Throughout much of the twentieth century, it was actively breeding and introducing new collards. Vates types are some of the most popular collards grown today. The first cold-resistant collard type introduced, today many Vates types are being bred for use around the world, especially as a winter crop. They have less waste (leaf to petiole ratio) and are slow to bolt in the spring, assuring an additional picking.

MASTERING COLLARDS

Collards prefer to grow in cooler weather. In warm climates, they are raised in the late autumn months or as a winter vegetable, while in cold climates they are best sown in June and allowed to mature in September. They are magnets for the typical host of brassica pests (mainly cabbage butterflies, cabbage moths, and cabbage loopers) but can grow relatively unharmed if raised under a floating row cover, at least until late autumn.

Rich soil, a constant supply of water, and stressless growing ensure the healthiest crop of leaves, and with collards, it's all about the leaves. While leaves can be swiped from the bottom of the plant, working up, the choicest leaves are often those closest to the crowns, which creates a dilemma about when to harvest. Choosing a couple of leaves per plant, harvested halfway up, is a good compromise.

Home-raised collards are infinitely more tender than those found at markets. Most home growers who've never tried collards before are hooked once they attempt them, adding new varieties of heirlooms to their planting lists each year.

VARIETIES

'Flash' F1 hybrid (55 days)—Another new Vates type with gloriously dark leaves and white midribs. Tender even when mature, this is the variety often used for baby-leaf production on farms. Mature leaves can be harvested through the fall and into winter, even in cold climates. Disease-resistant.

'Champion' open-pollinated (60 days)—A common Vates type with large leaves and raised ribs. It is slow to bolt. Some plants will winter-over in mild climates for extra harvests in early spring, especially in warm climates.

'Ole-Timey Blue' open-pollinated heirloom (65 days)—A beautiful, violet-veined, dark-green leaf makes this heirloom practically ornamental in the garden. Donated to Seed Savers Exchange by Ralph Blackwell of Alabama, whose family kept and shared the seed for generations.

'Georgia-type' (80 days)—The classic old-fashioned collard green that can reach 36 inches tall and produce loads of large, flavorful leaves that are sweeter after a light frost.

'Tiger' F1 hybrid (50 days)—A fast and excellent midseason collard with exceptionally dark, bluish-green leaves that can be savoyed (puckered) like savoy cabbage.

OPPOSITE: 'Georgia Green' collards.

BRUSSELS SPROUTS

Brassica oleracea var. *gemmifera*

Love them or hate them, brussels sprouts have overcome a poor reputation and emerged as a food star. No longer boiling them into beige oblivion, we've learned how to eat them. Roasted with olive oil and sea salt, even shaved raw into a healthy salad, the brussels sprout has moved up on the favorite vegetable list for many people.

The brussels sprout itself originated sometime around the twelfth or thirteenth century. It's safe to say that the magic happened on a farm between France (Brittany) and Belgium, where they were known to be consumed. In Victorian England, cookbooks started to discuss their use in dishes, while in North America, agricultural societies and journals introduced many to the "thousand-headed cabbage," listing varieties that ranged in size from 1 foot tall to 4 feet tall. Old recipes advised the cook to boil the sprouts until soft and then reheat them in a sauce often based on butter or cream. Of course, the stinky, graying spheres became notorious on people's most-hated-food lists.

HOW TO GROW BRUSSELS SPROUTS

Instead of sowing seed in early spring, seedlings should be started in early summer, but no later

OPPOSITE: 'Red Rubine' brussels sprouts plants are attractive even without their sprouts. A bit later than green brussels sprouts, these are just beginning to set up sprouts in early fall.

than July 4th, or plants won't be able to mature enough to form sprouts. Resist buying brussels sprouts seedlings when buying bedding plants in the spring—this will be a waste of money and time. Regardless of how healthy they appear, it is too early, and I would be suspicious of "healthy-looking" brassicas that are available too early. Sowing seedlings is easy to do in extra cell packs left over from tomatoes or calibrachoa. Set out on a deck with fresh, soilless mix, the seedlings can grow uninhibited to the perfect size— with their first or second true leaf forming.

The ideal germination temperature for brussels sprouts is around 80°F. You might see gardeners sharing posts with photos showing their freshly sown brussels sprouts seeds as early as February. Just resist and celebrate your success later.

The real trick to growing spectacular sprouts is the combination of two environmental factors that causes heading—temperature and the increasing length of the night. As discovered in botanical studies, it is this ever-increasing length of night that stimulates the budding on brussels sprouts. If plants are still immature when this period arrives, or if they have been stressed by drought, lack of fertility, or root restriction, it's likely that no sprouts will form.

MASTERING BRUSSELS SPROUTS

Brussels sprouts require much the same treatment as late cabbage, broccoli, and cauliflower. Practice

'Hestia' F1 hybrid brussels sprouts look more like collards in August, but don't worry—they won't start forming round sprouts until late October, when the nights start getting longer.

VARIETIES

'Hestia' F1 hybrid (100 days)—This more recent AAS winner is a better choice than the previous AAS winner, 'Jade Cross'. A good choice for smaller gardens as it is more compact.

'Nautic' F1 hybrid (120 days)—Commercial market variety that has tall plants with large sprouts. Has good resistance to black rot and Fusarium yellows.

'Franklin' F1 hybrid (125 days)—A very tall plant with firm sprouts of a premium size. Often the variety sold as sprouts on the stalk at markets. Impressive in the garden.

RED BRUSSELS SPROUTS

'Falstaff' open-pollinated (102 days)—This newer variety of 'Falstaff' is less red and more bluish-violet with some green. Its flavor is supreme, and it tends to hold its purple color when cooked more than does 'Rubine'.

'Rubine' open-pollinated (95 days)—The most commonly found red brussels sprouts. All red brussels sprouts tend to form smaller sprouts than green varieties, but often have more flavor.

'Red Bull' open-pollinated (90 days)—A dark-red variety with a milder flavor, it tends to hold its color better when cooked.

crop rotation if a brassica grew in the same location the previous year. Cabbage root maggot larvae that hatch in September will pupate near the base of any brassica, and be ready to emerge from the soil in the early spring.

PREPARING THE BED

Controlling disease and insects is key with brassicas, and even though the sprouts on brussels sprouts come late in the season, larvae can still be a problem. The use of plastic sheet mulch is advisable, as with all brassica crops. Tilling soil is also recommended with brassicas, as it will reduce the activity of cutworms. Few universities suggest using collars anymore and instead have gone back to recommending tilling. A tilled row garden like the one described in the section on kale (see page 65) is perfect for brussels sprouts.

Fertility is important for brussels sprouts, which need rich soil and proper pH between 7.0 to 7.8. Lime is essential to raise soil to near alkaline levels. The lime aids the plants in accessing the proper elements, and it maintains ideal soil conductivity, which can change, especially if you use organic fertilizer. An inorganic 10-10-10 feed can be sprinkled in before turning the soil—use about 2 cups per 4 × 8-foot bed. Cover with plastic mulch.

Set plants into the plastic by cutting a hole every 24 inches on a grid. Firm them in tightly and then water them with a booster feed (don't hate me, but one that is blue and high in nitrogen will get you to the state fair). A floating row cover applied immediately after planting is strongly recommended to reduce any impact from cabbage butterflies, cabbage moths, cabbage loopers, and flea beetles.

STARTING FROM SEED

Start seeds outdoors 4 months before first frost. In cold climates, this is usually around mid-June. By then the soil is warm enough to direct-sow outdoors if weeds are not a problem (2 to 3 seeds every 6 inches, later thinning plants to 18 to 20 inches). You could also start seeds outdoors in large cell packs or 3-inch pots, transplanting directly into a prepared bed by early July. Seed germination temperature is the same as for cabbage and other brassicas—near 80°F.

The plants should grow large and lush throughout the summer, and won't start forming sprouts until the days are shorter and the weather begins to cool down. The harvest season is long, starting after the first hard frost and often lasting until midwinter. Some growers pull the plants (complete with roots and mature sprouts) and set them in a damp, cold cellar or root cellar—especially growers who live in an area where winters are harsh and snow is deep.

Once frost nips the air, the flavor of brussels sprouts improves, typically around November.

ASIAN BRASSICA GREENS

Brassica rapa var. *japonica*, *B. rapa* var. *chinensis*, *B. rapa* var. *perviridis*, *Brassica rapa* var. *rosularis*

As home cooks become more adventurous with their ingredients, the idea of raising fresh Asian greens at home is becoming less novel every year. No longer considered exotic fare, many of the same Asian greens found in the produce aisle of the supermarket can easily be raised in the home garden.

Asian greens within the brassica family have a secret—they can all be sown in late summer and deliver fresh crops for dishes like stir-fries and soups in barely a month's time. Like all brassicas, the quality of home-grown Asian greens is practically immeasurable when compared to any found in local stores. Sweet, crispy, tender, and bright green, they are worth trying, especially as most gardeners will have excess space in the garden once the tomatoes and zucchini have been pulled for the season.

Depending on the size of the crop, most Asian greens found in seed catalogs can be grown in raised beds or elevated beds easily. Seed can be sown in early September in cold climates. I sometimes use extra flats with 2-inch pots left over from annuals earlier in the season, and then sow two seeds each of various bok choi, gai lan, and tatsoi. Seeds covered with ¼ inch of soil will germinate in a few days given that it is late summer.

Once seedlings grow to a size that is transplantable (usually the second pair of true leaves), I transplant them carefully into various vacant garden beds. These will last me until winter, especially if covered with a cold frame or floating row cover. Their culture and season, as well as their rate of growth, are very similar to that of napa cabbage.

The shortening days of autumn encourage dense growth, which you will notice immediately if you have tried to raise any of these crops in the springtime—spring-sown greens are more likely to bolt with the lengthening days of early summer. In fall, the season encourages ease of growth, and many of the greens are less bothered by insects, especially if planted in a sterile potting mix and raised in an elevated bed.

OPPOSITE: Quick-growing tatsoi and napa cabbage offer a gap-filling option for the colder autumn months, even growing in containers where tomatoes and peppers once grew in August. All this from seed sown in September.

VARIETIES

'Koji' F1 hybrid (35 days)—A tatsoi that is versatile. Can be raised as a baby green in mesclun mixes or as a stand-alone crop. For full-sized heads, space plants 8 inches apart in raised beds or 12 inches apart if setting out into the garden.

BOK CHOI (*BRASSICA RAPA* VAR. *CHINENSIS*)

'Black Summer' F1 hybrid (45 days)—An all-green bok choi highly resistant to bolting and designed especially for fall and early winter crops. Larger plants than most; space at 12 inches.

'Mei Qing Choi' F1 hybrid (45 days)—A very cold-tolerant green bok choi that grows a few inches shorter than 'Black Summer'. Good for raised beds.

'Shiro' F1 hybrid (30 days)—The tiniest baby bok choi that is miniature even when full-grown. Must be raised as a fall crop only, or it will bolt. Crisp, white stems and dark-green leaves.

MIZUNA (*BRASSICA RAPA* VAR. *JAPONICA*)

'Red Kingdom' F1 hybrid (40 days)—A beautiful dark-red mizuna-type Japanese mustard for bunching. Solid (not dissected) leaves. An AAS winner, it is sure to become a hit with home gardeners. I think it is more tender than other mizunas.

'Mizuna' open-pollinated (35 days)—The classic toothed-leaf Japanese mustard often found in mesclun mixes but rarely in markets because it wilts quickly. Sharp mustardy flavor like horseradish—a favorite fall treat for many.

KOMATSUNA (*BRASSICA RAPA* VAR. *PERVIRIDIS*)

'Carlton' F1 hybrid (35 days)—The standard Japanese braising green also used in broths and soups. The mild radishlike flavor is sharper if grown under warmer conditions.

BEETS, SWISS CHARD, AND SPINACH

Closely related botanically, beets, chard, and spinach each share similar cultural traits when grown in the garden. Not only are they able to germinate in cool, damp spring soil, but the young plants are also cold tolerant. This makes them suitable as winter crops in mild climates or crop extenders for use in winter hoop house culture in colder planting regions. Recently, the immature greens of both beets and chard have begun to enjoy a new purpose as young greens in spring and mesclun mixes, while continuing to be raised as productive crops and allowed to mature. Beets, chard, and spinach are some of the most nutritious crops a home gardener can grow.

BEETS
Beta vulgaris

Beets are an old-fashioned vegetable with vibrant color and edible greens that were one of the first vegetables consumed by humans. Beet greens are essentially the same as swiss chard, and the two are closely related botanically. Enjoyed by both the Romans and the early Greeks, beets were everyday fare throughout medieval Europe, particularly in Russia, eastern Europe, and Germany. Their earliest forms were carrotlike taproots with long, thick, stumpy roots. The selection process eventually led to other colors, shapes, and types.

It is said that nearly 20 percent of the world's sugar now comes from sugar beets. Even table beets have one of the highest sugar contents among vegetables, which is saying something for a root that some believe tastes like dirt.

Beets are an essential part of the home vegetable garden. They offer a long season of harvest, first as greens or baby beets, and then as a cold-hardy root that has many uses in the kitchen.

As with kale, the beet is experiencing a resurgence in popularity that is to a large extent health-based. It is a delicious root vegetable often roasted and included in salads, pickled, served as a side dish, or used as a base for classic eastern European soups like borscht.

CULTURE

Beets are relatively easy to grow in the home garden if you can offer them what they need. While direct-seeding into the garden in rows is an effective way to sow beets, you can find beet transplants at garden centers more frequently these days.

If you want to start beet seeds early, use a cell tray with 1-inch cells. It will start 150 plants for the cost of a seed packet. Seed can be started indoors under lights 5 to 6 weeks before the last heavy frost date. Transplant seedlings 4 to 6 inches apart in raised beds, either in grids or through a plastic sheet mulch that has had holes pierced in it—a very effective way to keep weeds down. Test your soil to ensure that the soil pH is higher than 6.0, as beets prefer a slightly alkaline level.

Beets grow best either in early spring or as a fall crop, but they should be pulled before a hard freeze. Plastic mulch will aid in maintaining soil moisture—any fluctuations can cause scabbing on the roots (woodiness). You can sow directly into the garden as well, spacing the rows 18 to 24 inches apart and mulching with straw between the rows to help control weeds. Thin the seedlings to 4 to 6 inches apart while young, and use the baby beets for pickling and the immature greens in smoothies or salads.

PESTS

The leaf miner is a common pest that causes grayish-brown paths in the foliage. The use of a floating row cover will help keep insects from laying eggs. Cercospora leaf spot can also be problematic. It is best resolved by practicing good crop rotation.

OPPOSITE: Conical beets such as these 'Cylindra' beets are old fashioned yet surprisingly practical as they make for more uniform slices and offer more beet per root.

VARIETIES

'Cylindra'—An old-fashioned long beet, excellent for pickling or slicing even rounds.

'Moneta'—A unique mono-seeded beet. Most beets have multiple embryos, which can cause duplication as seeds stick together once dried. Moneta contains only a single embryo, eliminating the need for thinning.

'Red Ace' F1 hybrid—A classic conventional variety.

'Bull's Blood'—The classic heirloom red-leaved variety for microgreens.

'Merlin' F1 hybrid—A new cercospora-resistant variety like 'Red Ace'.

'Chioggia'—The classic Italian white- and red-striped beet.

'Boldor'—Golden beet.

'Touchstone Gold'—Bright green leaf stems (petioles) and leaves complement these brilliant gold beets.

BELOW AND OPPOSITE TOP LEFT: Beets can tolerate transplanting, so start them early in plug flats. **OPPOSITE TOP RIGHT:** The foliage on some beets, such these 'Bull's Blood' beets, makes them popular for use in containers and ornamental beds. **OPPOSITE BOTTOM LEFT:** Candy-striped 'Chioggia' beets are beautiful alongside other midsummer beets from the garden. **OPPOSITE BOTTOM RIGHT:** The longer roots of 'Cylindra' beets were once common in the nineteenth century but are becoming popular again.

SWISS CHARD

Beta vulgaris subsp. *vulgaris*

One of the few pick-and-come-again vegetables you can grow in the garden, swiss chard provides a long season of harvest. Harvesting can begin as early as the baby chard stage at about 1 month, but can last as late as the end of the season, near frost in cold climates.

If you couldn't guess by looking at it, swiss chard is a beet. Not just related, it shares the same genus and species—*Beta vulgaris*. It's just a selection that doesn't form a thick root. Easy to grow (it's much easier than beet root), swiss chard is highly recommended for first-time gardeners and children. The plants are lovely, especially the colorful varieties such as 'Bright Lights' or any of the types sold simply as "rainbow chard."

GROWING SWISS CHARD

Swiss chard seeds are large, yet like beet seeds, they are comprised of a few seeds that are fused together. No worries though—thinning is easy later in the season, and then you can eat the younger thinnings. Some seed companies carry decorticated seeds—these have been processed a bit, or sanded down, which allows them to pass through automated seeding devices better. Sometimes this also breaks the seed up into single seeds, but there should be no concern either way, as seed clusters are normally only two or three seeds.

OPPOSITE: Rainbow chard, indeed. 'Bright Lights' is a variety that makes swiss chard look almost like candy.

Of all vegetables, swiss chard is perhaps the most versatile when it comes to temperature tolerance, but it does have its favored range, which leans toward the cool side. Germination is best if the daytime temperatures are in the 80s (86°F, to be precise). However, the seed can germinate in cold weather and can be sown when the outside temperatures are still around 40°F, just expect slower germination.

While seed and outdoor-raised seedlings can handle light frosts, young plants raised indoors are less tolerant. Transplant indoor-raised seedlings into the garden only after they have been acclimated (a week outside on a deck or terrace), and only once the weather has warmed.

Seeds can be started under lights indoors or in a bright, protected area outdoors, and moved in when below-freezing temperatures threaten—this is the ideal method. Seedlings can also handle transplanting well if you are gentle. Space plants 4 inches apart.

FERTILITY

Like most leafy greens, swiss chard grows to its finest when raised in rich, organic soils that have been amended with plenty of well-rotted manure and compost. Chard is a nitrogen lover, so a sidedressing of a high-nitrogen fertilizer will ensure that you get a healthy harvest of large dark-green leaves for the kitchen. Many commercial growers spread manure on their

fields in the winter to ensure that there is plenty of rich, organic nitrogen available.

Swiss chard that has been underfed is pale and tough. Follow a strict fertilizer schedule if you want healthy, dark greens. Swiss chard responds best to inorganic fertilizer, especially in cool weather (organic feeds are ineffective in cold weather because the bacteria in the soil are less active until the soil warms). Once warm weather arrives (over 75°F), you can switch to an organic feed until cool autumn weather sets in. Remember that organic fertilizers act only in continually moist soils, so monitor irrigation.

Side-dress rows every 3 weeks with a ½-inch band of granular nonorganic fertilizer. A 10-10-10 balance is fine, but if you can only find a mixed ratio, look for one where the first number (nitrogen) is the highest. The ammonium/urea source found in the inorganic fertilizer is accessed quickly by swiss chard in cool soils, but it will leach faster as well. In summer the organic sources of nitrogen (ammonium nitrate, which is what fish emulsion is) will last longer in the soil, but doses should be tripled.

LEFT AND OPPOSITE: 'Rhubarb' chard is an all-red type popular both in Europe and the United States.

VARIETIES

'Verde di Taglio' heirloom (35 days)—A true cut-and-come-again chard with spinachlike leaves. Considered very choice in Italy.

'Fordhook Giant' open-pollinated (40 days)—The standard large white-stemmed swiss chard with large savoyed leaves. Very tall.

'Bright Lights' open-pollinated (55 days)—A popular variety with rainbow-colored stems. AAS winner.

'Ruby Red' open-pollinated (50 days)—Red-stemmed, rhubarb-type chard. Good as a baby chard in spring salad mixes and also as a full-season chard.

SPINACH

Spinacia oleracea

Spinach is experiencing a new wave of appreciation thanks to several factors: baby spinach, the health movement, green shakes and smoothies, and new advancements in product packaging that now make greens available year-round. Not so long ago, there were only three ways to get it—canned, in a frozen wet block contained in a cardboard box, or tied in bundles of unwashed, mature spinach. Consuming fresh spinach meant time-consuming cleaning and the removal of bitter, tough stems, only to end up with that inescapable grit in your salad.

In the garden, spinach is a vegetable that transforms people, provided you can get past the labor and space required. Among the realities to face if you want to grow spinach, the most critical is that you must grow a lot of it.

Let's get one thing out of the way first—forget about growing baby spinach. It is a crop that is raised in hoop houses or greenhouses, sown thickly in wide bands that may reach 100 feet long or more. Special machinery has been designed to mow it like a lawn. If you sowed an entire 10-foot bed at home, the result of harvesting that bed at the baby spinach stage will be exactly one single bowl of cooked spinach.

Therefore, you have to ask yourself if spinach is worth growing. The answer is, "Certainly." Just be prepared for a few challenges.

HOW TO GROW SPINACH

Like peas, spinach demands cool weather. It's a classic early spring to early summer crop in cold climates, and a great fall one as well. In warmer climates you can grow spinach as a fall or winter crop. If you grow it in raised beds, prepare an entire bed. If sowing in rows or bands, or if broadcasting as you might grow a lawn (my preferred method), you will need at least ¼ pound of seed. Obviously, the small packets of seed sold at garden centers are impractical if you want to have enough spinach to cook. Raw spinach will go a bit further.

Soil pH is critical with spinach, perhaps more critical than with any other crop. Spinach will do little in the garden if the soil pH is 6.0 or lower. It prefers alkaline soils near 6.8 to 7.8. Spinach won't tolerate acidic soils, where there will tend to grow spindly and weak. If you love spinach and want to grow it well, invest in a home soil-test kit to use exclusively on spinach beds. In many gardens, the soil will need to be amended with dolomitic ground limestone (the powdered form and not the pelletized lime sold for lawns, as that is slow-acting). Spinach is a high-nitrogen feeder, as it is a leafy crop. Crops grow best in soils that are rich, with excellent moisture retention that will encourage quick growth and better access to nutrients.

Spinach can be sown directly into the cold soil as soon as you can prepare a bed in late winter or early spring. In warmer weather (above 85°F), germination can be erratic or even stop. If sowing a fall crop, keep an eye out for temperature shifts and time your planting accordingly.

Never sow spinach seeds in pots or cells. Sow seed directly in cool soil and never move a plant. Spinach can be raised in containers as a crop, however, and it grows well in elevated beds filled with a soilless medium but be sure to add lime to any mix containing peat, as it will be too acidic. Thinned seedlings can be used as baby spinach.

Since growing spinach in the garden is all about efficiency and yield, the larger 'Bloomsdale'-type of spinach is a great choice because it can remain in the ground longer, gradually growing into larger plants even as you steal a few leaves and stalks. The stalks of home-grown spinach are rarely tough, but often as tender as the leaves, and since you are the one managing the harvest, there is little chance of sand entering the bowl. I highly encourage everyone to try growing spinach to maturity, as so few have ever enjoyed the pleasure of a velvety soft

VARIETIES

'Kolibri' F1 hybrid (30 days)—A new, quick-growing savoyed-leaf spinach highly resistant to downy mildew.

'Kookaburra' F1 hybrid (26 days)—Very quick-growing savoy type for fast early spring crops. Disease-resistant hybrids are best for closely planted beds and hoop houses.

'Reflect' F1 hybrid (24 days)—Fast-growing variety with oval leaves for both spring and fall crops. Great as baby spinach if planting a big bed.

'Bloomsdale' open-pollinated (30 days)—Classic old variety with huge savoyed leaves and long stems. A larger spinach often preferred by spinach aficionados.

bowl of dark green freshly steamed spinach just from the garden. The 'Bloomsdale' types produce the largest mature plants with dark-green puckered leaves that are sometimes as large as leaf lettuce; newer varieties of spinach have been selected to have smoother leaves.

As a late-fall or even a winter crop, spinach excels. Some gardeners grow it under small hoops with row covers designed for winter culture, or perhaps more often in elevated cold frames. There are many ways to grow late-fall and winter crops today, and spinach is perhaps the most cold-hardy of them all. Even in cold climates, you can have spinach throughout much of the winter, often free from pests that can plague a spring crop. Overall, the most common pest that attacks leaf spinach is the leaf miner, whose small, beige, winding trails are a sure sign that larvae are tunneling through leaf layers. The use of floating row covers will help eliminate this annoying pest.

LEFT AND OPPOSITE: While baby spinach is now more common, larger 'Bloomsdale' types are best for home gardeners who need larger plants and larger yields. Homegrown spinach is infinitely more flavorful than store-bought, but it does take plenty of space.

5

THE LETTUCES

The lettuce family is more commonly known as the sunflower or thistle family because it is composed of what gardeners know of as the daisies, or thistles. It all has to do with how the petals are arranged. These "composit" (Compositae or Asteraceae) plants include some of the most common vegetables, yet we rarely think of them as relatives. If only we allowed the artichokes, cardoons, chicories, endives, and lettuces to flower, then their secret relations would be revealed—if not by their prickly personalities, then surely by their blossoms.

LETTUCE

Lactuca sativa

Few vegetable crops have undergone such an extensive cultural transformation in the past century as lettuce. When it comes to addressing lettuce, however, you cannot begin without considering the history of salad.

Historically, lettuce has been with us since at least the time of the Egyptians. Tomb paintings show what is believed to be early types of stem lettuce or romaine. Botanists theorize that most of today's edible lettuce originated in the Fertile Crescent—early Mesopotamia and the arable land around the Nile River. Considered eastern Mediterranean in its earliest form, the genus *Lactuca* is large, yet it is not global. Its more than 300 species are mostly found in Africa and western Asia.

LOOSE LETTUCE AND BABY LETTUCE

Anyone who was raised on the many fine varieties of lettuce that can be picked straight from the home garden knows that there is a vast world of salad greens to be enjoyed. Until the late twentieth century, lettuce was limited to a few supermarket types, mainly romaine, Boston, butterhead, oakleaf, and iceberg types. Mesclun changed this when it suddenly appeared on the scene in a big way.

RAISING LETTUCE FROM SEED

The most beautiful and highest-quality lettuce crop will come from seed you start at home. There are several reasons for this, but it begins with the varieties you choose, as today there are countless new varieties that have been improved tremendously. The most common struggle when starting lettuce seedlings at home is that they tend to be weak and limp under artificial light, but lettuce is quick enough to sow directly outside, even in early spring.

The trick to growing great lettuce at home is choosing where and when to sow your lettuce seed. Lettuce seed does not germinate well under lights because of "thermal dormancy." It germinates best near 50°F. It especially lags along when temperatures rise above 75°F. Cool soil temperature suits lettuce, and while it germinates optimally at just below 60°F, it often germinates very well when nights dip to 38°F as well.

I sow lettuce seed in what are essentially mini nurseries—a set of short bands or rows tucked somewhere into the garden either near the house in an elevated cedar bed with a twin-wall cold frame lid, or on the edge of a raised bed. This only requires a few scratches with a tine and a few rows a foot long, one for each variety sprinkled in. The

OPPOSITE: As the needs of restaurants and chefs' specialty markets demand premium varieties that look attractive on the plate, the 'Salanova' series delivers appeal on every level. 'Salanova Red Butter' might be pricey to buy for your salad already grown, but the seed is available for anyone to grow via mail order. Why limit yourself to common varieties when these are available?

seeds in this out-of-the-way nursery will germinate in a couple of weeks, even if sown just as the ground is defrosting. As you plant, be sure to keep track of the rows by adding waterproof labels.

Another optional planting method is to sow a pinch of seeds in cells or flats filled with a sterile soilless mix, then set out, perhaps with a cover, on a deck or terrace where you can keep an eye on them. Remove the clear cover if it gets too warm once the seedlings emerge.

These outdoor-raised plants will quickly outperform any store-bought seedling. They will be remarkably stocky and robust, able to withstand weather fluctuations that can plague other crops, such as late snowstorms and cold, heavy spring rains.

Lettuce raised outdoors can be transplanted easily, as lettuce tolerates some root disturbance while it is still young. Lettuce plants tend to mature at the same time, so resist planting your whole crop at once, and always save some seed for later in the summer. Sow thinly, as you may only need 8 or 10 plants of each variety. I like to sow successive crops every 3 weeks. Mini lettuce types (including many of the very fancy 'Salanova' strains) can be sown biweekly in higher numbers and are so pretty in the garden that a bed could almost be considered ornamental if they didn't look and taste so well. An entire bed gridded out with a matrix of various lettuce varieties is a beautiful sight.

FERTILITY

Lettuce is another crop that responds well to fertilizer (especially liquid feed) and rich soils with added organic matter like composted manure. A heavy nitrogen feeder, the combination of aged manure and liquid feed satisfies lettuce's need for a consistent supply of nutrients.

TOP: 'Salanova' varieties can be planted closer together because they form smaller heads, which make them ideal for containers. Baby 'Salanova' is set out here in a cold frame as a winter crop. **LEFT:** 'Dragoon' is a compact mini green romaine that remains crisp and sweet, even during hot summers.

LEFT TO RIGHT: 'Sylvesta' Boston-type, 'Cegolaine' Little Gem-type, and 'Salanova Green Sweet Crisp'.

The genetic diversity in lettuce is immense, which makes sense given its history of use in the human diet. The variation in cultivated lettuce was discovered to be so broad that taxonomists grouped them into seven types or genotype groups. Some of the following names will be familiar to both gardeners and cooks. These groups are helpful to know—especially if you are looking for particular characteristics in the lettuce that you wish to grow. The groups are:

1. Crisphead—An easy-to-remember group as these are primarily heading types of lettuce. Think iceberg or the larger semi-heading true Batavian types.

2. Butterhead—These lettuce varieties are distinguished by looser heads that remain soft and tender and are often described as having an oily texture. They include buttercrunch, gem types, deer tongue, Boston types, and bibb types. There are many additional varieties within the butterhead group.

3. Romaine or Cos—Generally upright in habit, romaine heads of lettuce have a distinct shape that most people are familiar with. There are both green and red varieties, some of which form a looser, elongated head.

4. Leaf—Open, loose heads commonly seen in gardens, such as oakleaf types or salad bowl types. Ruffled and lobed leaves in very loose rosettes or heads, they are good choices for warm summer harvests.

5. Latin, Batavian, or Summercrisp—This category includes loose-growing heads that look somewhat like a cross between a romaine and a butterhead. This category includes some important landrace varieties such as 'Grasse de Morges'—a regional variety shared among a few growers in France—along with many flavorful and crisp varieties that are relatively new, such as the 'Salanova' strain.

6. Stem—Stem lettuce, or asparagus lettuce, includes types similar to primitive romaine. Grown for their thick, crisp stems, they are commonly known as celtuce.

7. Oilseed—This is a popular type of lettuce in the Middle East and the western Mediterranean, where lettuce oil is commonly used in local cuisine.

CELTUCE

Celtuce is an unfamiliar vegetable to many people. It's hardly new but has taken its own sweet time in gaining visibility. Many might recall seeing it in seed catalogs, featured occasionally as a novelty crop. It may be portrayed as a sort of cross between celery and lettuce, or as asparagus crossed with lettuce. It is neither. Celtuce is true lettuce from head to toe, closely related to romaine, but in many ways more productive and even easier to grow. A more proper way to refer to it comes courtesy of the Chinese, who call it "stem lettuce," which is precisely what it is.

A true subspecies of what we know of as common lettuce (*Lactuca sativa* var. *augustana* to be exact), celtuce will change your mind about odd vegetables as soon as you taste it. In fact, I've never found anyone who dislikes it. After all, who can hate a crisp-as-a-water-chestnut vegetable that is also the color of pure jade? The main reason to grow celtuce is that it is addictive, and that's a very good thing when it comes to healthy vegetables. It will quickly enter your rotation of vegetables and kids even love it, particularly if added to stir-fries. It's a texture-thing.

The origin of celtuce is well documented, as types of stem lettuce are known to date back to the early Greeks and Romans. Images of stemmed lettuce appear in artwork found on their tombs, some dating as far back as 4500 BC. An interesting fact about these romaine types of lettuce is that they all produce a bitter, white latex sap—especially those closer to the wild lettuce species. This sap is proven to resemble that of the opium poppy. Of course, this feature has been bred out of modern selections, but it may explain why wild-derived stem lettuce was so popular with early cultures.

As stem lettuce moved into the New World, it was renamed to sound more appealing. It appears in mid-nineteenth-century seed catalogs as "asparagus lettuce" because seedsmen were trying to market it as a replacement for asparagus. In fact, when peeled, its shape and flavor are similar to asparagus, but its texture is much closer to a water chestnut. I personally would never associate it or confuse it with asparagus. Most will think that a slice of it is closer to the texture of a water chestnut but the color of jadite sea glass. It seems to have everything going for it except a good name and a PR agent.

Stem lettuce has never been popular in Western gardens, but not for lack of effort. A Mennonite farmer named Jacob B. Garber is said to have cultivated the first plants of celtuce in Lancaster County, Pennsylvania, in the 1850s. In Europe, a similar story prevailed, especially in France, where it remained in catalogs longer than in North America. The mid-nineteenth-century French grew celtuce in their gardens for more than 30 years after it had disappeared from American seed catalogs.

Celtuce reappeared in 1897, billed as asparagus lettuce in the spring issue of *Dreer's Garden*

Calendar. Dreer's wrote that "this new vegetable originated from France" but did not mention China at all. It was discontinued the following year and remained absent from Western gardens, except when cultivated by early Chinese immigrants, who grew it on farms in California and Arizona. The last big launch came in 1942, when the W. Atlee Burpee Company rebranded stem lettuce with the name celtuce. This was the first time most people had heard of celtuce, and the Burpee story was more elaborate. Their seeds were reportedly acquired from a missionary in China, the Rev. Carter D. Holton, who wrote in 1938 that he enjoyed the vegetable near the Tibet border, later delivering seeds to Mr. Burpee in 1940 to field-test.

Ruth Reichl, a former editor of *Gourmet* magazine, discovered a brief story in a 1942 *Gourmet* issue mentioning that celtuce was indeed the new vegetable awaiting rediscovery. The article described an elegant dinner party at the posh Waldorf-Astoria Hotel: "Celtuce vinaigrette was served at a festive dinner Lucius Boomer, president of the Waldorf-Astoria, gives annually to the hotel and nightclub managers of New York City." The article also mentioned that the vegetable was being grown in the western states at that time.

Today, many are rediscovering this delightful and easy-growing vegetable outside of China. You won't find it yet at your average supermarket, but it can be found nearly year-round at larger Asian grocers.

HOW TO GROW CELTUCE

Like so many vegetables, homegrown is considerably better, and this premise holds true with celtuce—home-raised stems will be even more crispy, more flavorful, and intensely greener once peeled and sliced. Store-bought celtuce tends to be yellowish or pale greenish-white. One of the exceptional characteristics of this vegetable is its lovely jade color when sliced.

Sow celtuce seed early. Like all lettuce, its germination rates are highest in colder temperatures, ideally around 40°F. Sow seed in cells or flats that you can set outdoors in early spring, as temperature swings will also stimulate germination. If you are starting seed indoors, cover seed with ¼ inch of vermiculite. Set trays or cells in a cool, bright location. If using grow lights, raise them higher to keep the seed trays cool. Harden indoor seedlings by reducing watering 3 to 4 days in advance of planting outdoors. The brightest light and coolest temperatures will help keep seedlings stocky. Established and hardened seedlings can handle moderate frosts and even temperatures down to 20°F for brief periods.

Constant moisture is essential with any lettuce crop, but even more so with celtuce as the stem must remain turgid. Even well-watered plants will wilt on hot days, but this causes no lasting damage as they will recover by evening. A watering via a drip hose or sprinkler in the early morning during summer should suffice. Prolonged dry spells followed by deep irrigation, however, can cause problems with celtuce, as the stems can become hollow. This is merely a cosmetic inconvenience, but one to be avoided. More worrisome is stem-splitting, which may occur with irregular watering and which will encourage decay in warm weather. Check plants often once they elongate into tall plants, as splitting can happen just as the crop is ready to be harvested. It is especially common after a sudden rainstorm that follows a prolonged drought. Harvest plants by pulling them out by their roots, removing the root ball and the leaves with a knife. Early morning is best. Washed and cleaned stems with their skin still on will last 3 to 4 weeks if kept in a zip-top bag in the fridge.

TOP: Sow celtuce, just like lettuce, indoors in early spring. **ABOVE:** Celtuce transplants easily; grid seedlings 10 inches apart. **OPPOSITE:** Freshly pulled celtuce stems in early July are ready for the kitchen. Just peel and slice the crispy jade-like stems into your favorite stir-fry or brothy soup.

Mulching is not recommended for celtuce, as it encourages both pathogens and excess moisture near the stem base. If you do decide to mulch, weed-free straw or salt-marsh hay is better than plastic, as it can breathe. Keep mulch clear of the stem base. Frequently hand-cultivate the top 2 inches of soil with a Dutch hoe to create a dry crumb layer between the damp soil below and the plant above. Celtuce has a large footprint, with each plant consuming 4 square feet when it is mature. Judicious spacing at 1½ to 2 feet apart will ensure that individual plants have enough room, and will encourage air circulation. A 4 × 10-foot row can bear 20 plants.

MASTERING TECHNIQUES

Some elevated cedar planting beds have a twin-wall greenhouse cover that essentially converts the bed into an elevated cold frame. This is ideal for growing celtuce and other lettuces, as it can be opened on warm, sunny days and closed on the most frigid early spring days. Once seedlings form their second or third pair of leaves, they can be lifted and relocated to a prepared bed in the garden to mature.

VARIETIES

Varieties are few, with only a few available in North American and European seed catalogs. Online sources for Asian seed suppliers do offer more, but be wary of private sellers, as they can be less reliable when it comes to authenticity in variety.

'Spring Tower'—The recommended variety for home growers in North America.

'Red-Stem'—A choice dark red–leaved variety popular throughout much of China but challenging to find in the west. Look for seed online listed as 'Wosun'.

'Tianjin Big Stem'—A popular commercial variety in China. It forms stems as thick as 3 inches and tolerates warmer weather.

'Summer 38'—A Chinese-bred selection less likely to bolt in hot weather.

'Angustana'—Appears to be synonymous with celtuce varieties, as *augustana* and *angustata* are subspecies names.

OPPOSITE: Celtuce plants grow quickly in late spring with lots of water.

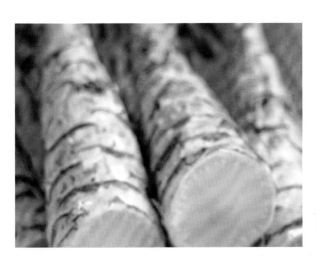

ENDIVE AND CHICORY

Cichorium endivia, C. intybus

You are not alone if you are confused about what is and what isn't considered endive, escarole, or chicory. Botanically speaking, the vegetables we know best are from just two species of chicory. *Cichorium endivia* includes curly-leaved varieties like frisée, and some very lettuce-looking types we know as escarole. Other related varieties (*Cichorium intybus*) form heads and are typically forced in winter, like witloof (which means white-leaved) or Belgian endive, as well as many Italian radicchios.

Only a generation ago, the bitter greens of endive and escarole were enjoyed almost exclusively by those of Italian or Mediterranean ancestry. Today, various types of chicory, endive, and escarole can be found just about everywhere, primarily in bagged mesclun mixes. There is tremendous diversity in this group of greens, from the 1970s salad bar standards like curly endive to the frisées and radicchios that have sneaked into our kitchens in much the same way as arugula.

Most people today can identify at least some types of endive and escarole. Red radicchio can hardly be considered exotic anymore, as it is a common ingredient in bagged salad mixes. But home cooks and gardeners rarely

OPPOSITE: Forcing your own Belgian endives in January may seem tedious, but not only is it highly cost-effective, it's also surprisingly easy.

consider adding any of the endives or escaroles to the home garden. This is unfortunate, as the leafy types are quick-growing fall crops that can last long into the colder months and tolerate frost and freezes.

HOW TO GROW

Leafy varieties not intended to be forced, such as escarole and frisée, are best grown as fall crops. Order seeds by mid-July for sowing anytime from late July to mid-August.

Sow three or four seeds in individual cell containers filled with a sterile potting mix, thinning to a single plant once they germinate. Set the trays in a spot where you won't forget to water them. A protected spot near the foundation of the house or on the deck is often a good choice. Seedlings will grow quickly in midsummer and will appreciate a feed with a water-soluble fertilizer, such as fish emulsion, to keep them growing without stress. As soon as the first leaves appear, thin seedlings to a single plant per cell and consider your options of where you might plant them. Even ornamental container plantings can benefit from a few endive or escarole plants to balance out fall displays of chili peppers and kale. Or you might want to replace a fading row of beans or peas with frisée or endive. You may be surprised to see how well these plants produce as the days grow shorter and chilly night temperatures arrive. Leafy greens will mature by late October, and in mild seasons can be harvested until the holidays or longer if protected.

HARVEST

Most endives are loose heads with a distinctive bitter snap. To both tenderize and blanch the inner leaves, the outer leaves can be tied up with twine around October 1, or when the plants are large and floppy. This will improve the quality of frisée, but some people enjoy the bitterness of escarole left untied and un-blanched, for a few inner leaves will naturally become pale as the plant matures. The old-fashioned method of laying boards atop rows to compact the crowns is now discouraged as it often induced decay, especially during fall rains and cool temperature. Frisée is a particularly pleasurable crop to grow as it is often difficult to find in markets, and when it is available, it can be expensive.

VARIETIES

DANDELION-TYPE CHICORIES

'Catalogna'—A true puntarelle type of chicory. Essentially a fancy dandelion that is raised for its crispy white stems. Puntarelle is highly valued in fine restaurants in Italy, where they are soaked until crisp and shredded into thin slices with a special wire tool called a puntarelle slicer.

'Rossa Italiana'—A red-stemmed dandelion green beautiful in salads when young.

'Barba di Cappuccino'—Also known as 'Monk's Beard'. A long, white-stalked dandelion with serrated leaves.

RADICCHIO

'Variegata di Castelfranco'—A lovely pale-green and red-striped heading radicchio from Italy.

'Variegata di Lusia'—Maybe the most sought-after radicchio by chefs. Nearly white leaves with red speckles and spots.

'Rossa Treviso sel Svelta' heirloom—Looks like a red and white witloof, but it doesn't need forcing. Sometimes it's sold in grocery stores in 3-packs along with romaine lettuce as it shares a similar shape.

FORCING ENDIVE

'Totem' F1 hybrid—The classic Belgian endive available now as an improved strain. Roots easily force in winter when brought out of refrigeration and set into pots of soil, then kept dark and warm until chicons form.

'Treviso Tardiva' heirloom—A red forcing endive with historic DOP (translated as "Protected Designation of Origin" in English) status in Italy, it can now be raised at home. Dig roots in autumn and force in pots in a warm, dark location.

'Rossa di Treviso' heirloom—The closest thing to a red Belgian endive. Can also be raised as a salad green when young.

LOOSE-HEAD ENDIVE

'Rhodos' open-pollinated—A nice fall salad green similar in style to Très fine Maraîchère, an heirloom French type of endive. Best as a fall crop.

'Dubuisson'—Known as a 'Wallonne' type (the common endive found in American supermarkets). Sharp foliage and tender, pale-yellow interior leaves surrounded by dark-green, finely indented outer leaves. Best grown for fall harvest.

ESCAROLE

'Natacha' open-pollinated—A standard new selection of escarole with flat, tender leaves, semi-heading into loose heads in autumn with attractive creamy-yellow hearts. Optimal as a fall crop.

ARUGULA

Diplotaxis tenuifolia

Arugula has taken the world by storm. Thirty years ago it was still considered a fancy Italian green that sometimes was added to mesclun mixes. Today arugula is often found growing in the raised beds of suburban gardens, and is even served in spring salad mixes found in high school cafeterias.

The peppery arugula, while botanically a brassica, is more often thought of as a salad green, so I include it here alongside its best friends: lettuce, endive, and mesclun mixes. As more and more people fall in love with arugula, more obscure varieties are turning up.

Arugula is perhaps the simplest crop to grow in the garden. In fact, of all the greens, it is quicker and more likely to succeed in almost any garden, although it enjoys the typical brassica treatment of rich, fertile soil and plenty of moisture and organic matter.

Pests usually aren't a problem, aside from flea beetles, which will chew tiny holes in the leaves. This rarely affects anything but their appearance. If grown with the right nutrients, arugula outperforms all spring greens. While it will often become too spicy in summer when it is warm, if kept well irrigated, successive crops can be had from earliest spring until late autumn, and even into winter if covered with fleece.

OPPOSITE: The *Diplotaxis* arugula species has toothed leaves, a stronger bite, and is more cold tolerant than *Eruca sativa*, the milder and wide-leafed variety shown here.

Sow seed thinly in bands 3 or 4 inches wide. Oversowing will result in yellowing leaves and plants that will need to be picked younger as they will go to seed sooner. Arugula grows so quickly that its window of opportunity is small—a couple of weeks, much like cilantro. This should remind us that those little 4-inch pots of arugula seedlings available at garden centers in the spring are a waste of money.

If arugula is left in the garden too long, plants will bloom within a month, and while the flowers too are edible, why waste the space? In a raised bed, it's smart to sow bands of arugula every week and a half, especially if you buy it at the market once a week. This should supply a family of four with the weekly amount you'd typically get in a poly box of spring greens.

Cut leaves off as needed or just shear with scissors directly from the row. Arugula also grows well in containers and elevated beds. Cold tolerant, the seed can be sown early in spring with temperatures around 40°F, or as late as 4 weeks before hard freezes arrive.

In warmer climates, it's the ideal winter crop, beginning with fall sowings that are repeated throughout the winter. Like mesclun, it also does well in window boxes and large containers, though it is not attractive enough to be considered ornamental, and these pots should be hidden in a kitchen garden area, as harvesting the greens with scissors can look untidy.

VARIETIES

'Astro' open-pollinated (38 days)—A large-leaved variety with oak-leaf-shaped leaves.

'Esmee' open-pollinated (28 days)—Attractive lobed leaves. Can be raised both as a baby-leaf crop and as a full-sized-leaf crop.

'Sylvetta' open-pollinated (50 days)—A "wild" type of arugula or rocket similar to types once foraged for in Italy. Deliciously strong flavor with finely cut leaves. Has yellow flowers rather than white.

'Wasabi' open-pollinated (45 days)—Not true wasabi of course (that's from the genus *Wasabia*), but a solid-leaf arugula with sinus-clearing hotness very similar to wasabi.

OPPOSITE BOTTOM: The *Eruca* species often sold as arugula grows better in spring and summer. It has broader leaves and foliage that is more tender. The lobing on the leaves can vary in shape.

MESCLUN

Mesclun, at least how we know it today, is a very recent invention, dating back only to the 1970s and 1980s. Mesclun means "mixture" and is basically a marketing term, although the idea of mesclun is in fact much older. Many food historians think it is based on "misticanza," a wild-green mixed salad originally made from leaves of bitter herbs and greens foraged from the fields in Provence.

Today mesclun is a kitchen staple that's served just about everywhere. Mesclun mixes are sometimes referred to as "classic Italian," which means they could contain any number of bitter greens, along with spicy ones. Bitter greens include endive and escarole, while the spicier greens comprise arugula, cress, and various mustards.

Mild mixes are predominantly made up of various types of lettuce, swiss chard, and spinach, but any number of varieties could be included, such as tatsoi, bok choi, orach, mizuna, and certain herbs such as dill.

It's fun to make your own mixes, and blending them is also a good way to use up excess seed at the end of the year. The trick with mesclun mixes is to choose varieties that will germinate roughly at the same time. A 'Bull's Blood' beet, for example, won't germinate as quickly as will red mustard. Group cool-germinating types separate from warm-germinating types as well.

Sow seed thickly, but try not to have seeds touching each other. I like to mix seed with some dry potting mix in a bowl and then sprinkle it onto a bed, usually in a wide band. I sow only half of a row at first, then the other half 2 weeks later in order to get a staggered harvest.

Most greens sprout quickly, and while they can be picked at any size, 3 to 4 inches is ideal. Use scissors to shear off what you need rather than trying to pick leaves one by one. The tight growing conditions will cause leaf yellowing and premature bolting before long, and it's easier to plant a band a few weeks later.

Keep the pickings in a large bowl and then fill it with cold water to rinse. Strain through a colander. Spread out leaves on a tea towel and roll it up, placing it in the refrigerator to crisp for at least an hour as mesclun benefits from some cool. Store unused washed mesclun in a plastic bag with a damp paper towel in it.

Mesclun is best grown in the early spring or early autumn and into winter. I start my first crops in March, sowing seed in covered cold frames. I also save a few jars of seed for seed flats that I can bring into the greenhouse throughout the winter. Most mesclun mixes are tolerant of cool weather.

OPPOSITE: Mesclun mixes can be purchased premixed, or try mixing your own from all the extra seed you haven't used. I keep a jar full of my favorite types of greens, including mustards, arugulas, cresses, and many types of lettuce seeds. Grow crops in flats or plug trays with a pinch of seeds in each and harvest as needed. Even under lights, a crop can be ready in just a month.

TOP: My homemade spicy mesclun mix is comprised of seeds that grow to a cuttable size around the same time. It includes various types of green and red mustard greens, Russian kale, cress, arugula, and Japanese mizuna. **BOTTOM:** Some mesclun mixes are comprised of just lettuce varieties. I often use leftover seed from the previous season, which I mix together and keep handy in a jar.

6

CARROTS, CELERY, AND PARSNIPS

The Apiaceae family is a diverse group of plants. Some, like carrots and parsnips, are edible taproots. Some, like celery, are raised for their edible stalks. Others are generally herbs that we cultivate to enjoy eating the leaves and small stems. As with just about any plants, you will have the best success by starting your own seeds. In many cases, that is the only option. Most of the plants in the carrot family do not take well to transplanting or any other form of root disturbance.

Succession planting is very important to maintaining a steady supply of herbaceous plants such as parsley and cilantro. This is especially true in the summer, when they grow much faster and are likely to bolt if you wait even a day too long to pick them.

While planting directly in the garden yields the best results, many of the carrot family plants can be grown quite successfully in containers. In fact, if you search seed catalogs you can usually find varieties that are selected precisely for their ability to adapt to container life.

CARROTS

Daucus carota subsp. *sativus, D. carota* var. *atrorubens*

The carrot may very well be the first vegetable that early humans domesticated. Native to the high mountains of the Middle East, Afghanistan, Iran, and Persia, the wild carrots of antiquity look nothing like the iconic orange taproots we know today.

Home-raised carrots excel in flavor, especially when compared to the mass-market carrots that may have spent as much as a year in storage. The scent of a freshly dug carrot is both earthy and sweet. Digging a fresh carrot is a ritual no gardener should miss, yet many still overlook the carrot when planning their garden.

Truth be told, raising carrots well in the home garden isn't particularly easy. Carrots are highly responsive to care, and they frequently are raised without attention to the simple details they require. Carrots are a long-season crop that depends on your understanding of their basic needs, including soil preparation, nutrition, specific watering needs, and sunshine. With carrots, it goes a step further, as you must also consider correct seeding and careful thinning of the young plants, as well as maintaining a consistent environment of constant moisture.

PLANTING AND CARE

Direct-sow carrots in the garden in spring or early summer. Sow them thinly in bands or rows,

BEHIND THE SCENES

You may notice that "baby carrots" do not appear as a type. That's because the so-called baby carrot is a modern invention marketed to children and dieters. The baby carrot is in fact an early-maturing Nantes type (sometimes known as Amsterdam type) that is harvested and then has the top 2 inches cut off. It is then tumbled to resemble a short, stumpy carrot. I am often asked how to raise baby carrots at home, and the good news is that there are new carrot varieties being introduced that mature more quickly. They still may not delight your kids, though, as their shape doesn't look anything like a packaged baby carrot. But if you allow your kids to grow and pick their carrots, they will learn that a carrot pulled straight from the garden is the sweetest of treats.

OPPOSITE: Carrots come in a rainbow of colors. Try them all and mix them up.

FENNEL

Foeniculum vulgare var. *azoricum*

Fennel is a classic Mediterranean herb that evolved through selection early on, as it was cultivated throughout much of southern Europe. It was lesser known in North America, however, until Italian immigrants began growing it in the early twentieth century. Even then, it never became popular until the late twentieth century in America.

Today fennel has a wide fan base, ranging from fine chefs to home cooks to foodies who enjoy its aniselike flavor. Anise seed and fennel seed have similar flavor profiles, although anise is sweeter. Both anise seed and fennel seed are used as the primary flavorings in absinthe. While true anise remains uncommon in vegetable gardens, it is a good addition to any culinary herb garden, if only for its seeds, but fennel will suffice, offering a similar flavor profile.

The plant called "wild fennel" also has an anise flavor, but it is of a different genus altogether. Wild fennel does not form a bulbous base on the stem but is still sometimes used as a flavoring.

Most fennel is biennial in nature. Some may appear perennial, but no vegetable gardener would attempt to keep fennel through to a second season—or at least they shouldn't, because fennel is classed as an invasive species in much of the world. Its seed heads should be properly destroyed, especially if you live in a mild climate like California. Many scientists agree that fennel is a true biennial, with some perennial traits in warmer climates, while some insist that it can behave much like an annual north of USDA Zone 4.

The medicinal properties of fennel remain an area of great interest to medical researchers. Phytochemically it is considered a powerhouse plant, and there are multiple studies and abstracts that list its potential benefits, with most of them focused on antioxidant properties and its unique ability to create phytoestrogens.

GROWING FENNEL TO PERFECTION

Homegrown fennel can be far better than any found in supermarkets, but there is no denying that it is challenging to grow well. Achieving the ideal fleshy, crisp, large bulb is tougher than you might imagine. The most common mistake made when growing fennel is planting at the wrong time. This can cause incorrect temperature exposure and day length issues. Because fennel is a biennial, it must be sown near the summer solstice. It should never be started early indoors or under artificial lights, as it can become confused vernally—its internal clock is very sensitive to day length and early exposure to cold temperatures in the spring.

The answer here is to sow fennel seed at the right time, which is once the weather has fully warmed up and the soil temperature is near 75°F. The good news is that fennel sown outdoors either in individual cell packs or spaced out in rows will be remarkably resilient, as long as the roots are never disturbed.

TROUBLESHOOTING PROBLEMS

If your fennel is prematurely sending up a stalk, there is no trick to stop it. Cutting the stalk off is ill-advised and will not stop the decline of the plant, nor will it stimulate the bulb to form earlier.

If your fennel begins to bloom and goes to seed before the end of summer, all is not lost. You may have failed for that one year at raising fennel bulbs, but there are other ways to save the crop. Just tell visitors that you are not growing fennel bulbs, but rather fennel pollen—an expensive ingredient that many chefs cherish. To gather fennel pollen, shake it from the bright-yellow umbels onto a clean linen sheet. Get a helper to hold the stems while someone else shakes the pollen off. Do this on a warm, dry afternoon, and save the pollen granules in an airtight jar for use in the kitchen. You can use it as a sprinkle for goat cheese or on any seafood dish that will benefit from the slight anise flavor it brings.

Fennel seeds are good to save as well (remember, fennel is considered an herb). Allow the seed heads to dry on the stems, and pick them while they are still green, but after any sign of pollen has passed. Cut the entire stalk and hang it to dry in a porch or breezeway. The dried stems themselves can also be saved and added to your grill fire to season fish just before serving (a classic French method especially favored with sole).

CULTURE

In the garden, fennel raised for its bulbs must be sown in warm soil near the summer solstice and allowed to grow without stress (lots of water and fertility) through the hot summer to maturity in the cool autumn. Varieties selected as bulbing types have swollen stems near the base that form the fleshy, crisp bulb structure.

Fennel seed requires complete darkness to germinate, so cover the seed with ½ inch of soil. Cell packs work well if one or two seeds are set into each individual cell, and the entire tray is set outdoors to grow in natural light. Once seedlings open their second pair of

VARIETIES

'Zefa Fino' open-pollinated (65 to 80 days)—An improved variety ideal for small market growers as well as the home garden. Can be harvested as baby fennel early in the season or mature fennel at 80 days.

'Montebianco' open-pollinated (65 to 70 days)—Medium-sized bulbs that mature earlier in the autumn.

'Mantovano' open-pollinated (75 to 85 days)—A premium Italian strain with the largest, whitest, and sweetest bulb. Long-season grower with a fine, crisp texture. Best quality comes from midsummer sowing for late-fall harvests.

'Fennel of Parma' ('Finocchio di Parma')—A choice market variety from Italy with the smallest bulbs that are nearly round. Bulbs are of a very fine and crispy quality often preferred by specialty markets and chefs.

'Bianco Perfezione Sel Fano' heirloom (80 to 85 days)—High sugar content and crispy white bulbs. Best grown as a fall crop. Popular in Italy.

'Romanesco' open-pollinated (85 days)—The classic heirloom variety most similar to the varieties found in markets in North America. Tight, wrapped stem bases and a large bulb base.

ferny leaves, they should carefully be slipped out of their pots and into a prepared bed.

If direct-sowing seed into a bed, take great care in thinning the row. Pull out seedlings that are too close together, tossing them or using them as microgreens in a salad. Resist the urge to transplant them again, as they will sulk and bolt given the root disturbance. Plants should be spaced at least 10 to 12 inches apart in rows that are 24 inches apart.

Fennel appreciates both high fertility and consistent moisture. Unlike carrots, fennel reacts positively to a fertilizer program that offers high nitrogen levels. The largest bulbs will come from crops that have been fed consistently with nitrogen (commercial growers use 21-0-0). Excellent results can be achieved by digging-in well-rotted cow manure before planting, or by applying liquid fish emulsion weekly. Side-dressing plants with a 20-5-5 fertilizer every 3 weeks gives them a beneficial shot of nitrogen during the summer.

Consistent watering is essential, as fennel (like celery) is 90 percent water. Maintain an irrigation system in which the beds receive the same amount of water each week (1 to 2 inches). Also water before any threat of drought occurs. Once fennel wilts it is too late, and the damage is irreversible.

PESTS AND DISEASE

Few pests other than aphids and the larvae of pollinators left on the foliage bother fennel in the home garden. With fennel, insect damage is usually limited to just the ferny foliage and is therefore mostly cosmetic. Black swallowtail larvae can be hand-picked off the plants and relocated if they bother you.

Aphids can be a problem early in the summer, but by late autumn the plants should be large enough to discourage aphids, which prefer tender new growth. If a serious outbreak occurs, *Bacillus thuringiensis* may be used, as aphid larvae are vectors for a few serious viruses that can damage other crops, particularly carrots.

Young or mature fennel harvested in fall pairs beautifully with heirloom russeted apples.

PARSNIPS
Pastinaca sativa

While not a common vegetable, the parsnip is a real old-timer. It is a classic, old-fashioned, long-season garden plant. In the northern climates, parsnips are known to be best if sown directly into the garden, always in earliest spring, and then harvested after the first hard frost.

When you see your first parsnip, you may think it's a white carrot, which isn't actually too far from the truth. They are from the same family. While they may seem hard to grow, parsnips are relatively low-maintenance, aside from occasional weeding. Much of the hard work happens up front with soil preparation.

Parsnip culture is straightforward for northern gardens: sow early when the soil is still cold, and always use the freshest seed possible as parsnip seed is short-lived. After that it's a waiting game. Parsnip seed is slow to germinate, taking as long as a month to emerge from the soil, when just a bit of a leaf can be identified. Old gardening books often suggest sowing a radish seed along with the parsnip to help mark where the seeds were sown.

In England, the parsnip is popular as a serious competitive vegetable. Growers there are fond of sharing their secrets and tips, as well as step-by-step tricks. The methods are daringly different, yet worth paying attention to if you are interested in improving your parsnip-growing skills. But be forewarned that many of the tricks are time-consuming and quite elaborate.

As with most root vegetables, soil preparation is the key to successfully growing parsnips. The primary goal is to create the ultimate obstacle-free course for the long roots to grow down into. Some growers use PVC pipes set into soil which are filled with sand or sifted potting mix. Seeds are sown on the surface, or young seedlings are carefully set into position, creating a deep, perfectly straight channel of obstacle-free growing medium.

I use a method that requires you to start parsnips indoors in deep seedling pots sometimes called root trainers. It allows perfectly straight roots to grow to a depth no greater than the dept of the pots. Then, the entire soil ball is transplanted into a prepared hole in the garden, into which potting soil has been added. The result: long and thick parsnips.

Usually, though, parsnips are raised without such elaborate care. They are simply sown directly into a tilled bed like carrots. This technique results in roots that have thick crowns but quickly taper to a stumpy root tap once extracted in the fall. These have little value in the kitchen.

Following are two methods I have found to work well. You can decide what works for you.

METHOD 1: CONVENTIONAL METHOD
Best results come from pelleted seed prepared in an inert, clay coating. Monitor the weather for the first few weeks as parsnip seed can take a month to germinate. Water the seeds in well.

CELERY

Apium graveolens

If you have ever tried to grow celery at home, the first question you may be asking now is this: Is celery worth growing in the home garden? A reasonable question. Anyone who has attempted to grow this challenging vegetable realizes that expecting results that come anything close to supermarket celery is unrealistic.

One of the most ancient vegetables, celery (or more accurately, its wild species) was found in the tomb garlands of the pharaoh Tutankhamun. It is thought that wild celery was most likely used as an herb throughout antiquity, and not consumed as a salad vegetable until less bitter selections were made in the mid-nineteenth century. Until then, it was the leaves and roots (celeriac) that made their way into the human diet.

Celery arrived in Europe relatively late, and by 1700 appeared in cookbooks as a type of parsley referred to as "smallage." It arrived even later into American gardens, only reaching popularity in the nineteenth century. Fearing Burr's *The Field and Garden Vegeta-*

bles of America (1863) lists 37 varieties including white, purple, and pink strains.

Home-raised celery is a bitter herb and a worthy vegetable for the intense flavor it contributes to soups, stocks, and stews. While achieving the thick, crispy, mild-flavored stalks of supermarket celery is almost impossible, the home chef will cherish its usefulness in many dishes.

Heirloom varieties can be grown in the same manner that celery was grown in the eighteenth and nineteenth centuries, but few gardeners today would bother. This method includes digging a trench 1 foot deep and 6 feet wide, and setting plants 9 inches apart in rows. The soil is then "earthed up" every 2 weeks until most of the plant is underground. This blanches the bitter compounds out of the stems and results in a pale stalk that was once cherished, as old varieties were extremely bitter.

In Victorian times, celery was left in the ground throughout the winter, becoming milder as the season progressed. Some farmers transplanted celery into hot beds (cold frames filled with fresh manure and then clean soil) with a covering of straw to force a luxury crop of blanched celery.

CULTURE

Celery has some unique concerns that must be addressed while it is young. Seeds sown ⅛ inch deep in plug trays filled with sterile soil mix make

OPPOSITE: Celery seedlings grow slowly at first, so an early sowing in late January is required. Once transplanted into cell trays by late February, plants will start to grow faster. Young plants must be kept warm (above 50°F) until the weather outdoors has warmed completely, or else they will vernalize (believing that they survived a mini-winter), resulting in plants that will bolt or go to seed. This is common with garden-center celery sold too early.

transplanting easier. Germination is slow: expect 2 to 3 weeks for emergence with bottom heat set at 75°F. Seedlings should be kept in bright light in a greenhouse, or under lights indoors at temperatures between 65°F and 72°F. Slow-growing at first, celery seedlings require patience.

High moisture and high fertility are key throughout celery's life, so keep the soil moist from sprouted seedling through harvest. Home gardeners should dig-in a granular 10-10-10 fertilizer at a rate of 6 pounds to every 100 square feet, with additional side-dressing every 3 weeks throughout the summer.

Pay close attention to keeping the bed well irrigated (2 inches of water a week). Never allow the bed to go completely dry, or plants may become stunted.

Many of us assume that celery is a cool-weather crop, and while it can stand a hard winter outdoors once mature, young plants must be treated with great care. Seedlings must never be exposed to cold temperatures, even after they are set out into the bed in mid-spring. A week of exposure to temperatures below 55°F can vernalize young plants, and they will bolt (go to seed). Celery is a biennial plant.

It may seem that there are few practical reasons to raise celery, but it is a rewarding vegetable if you have the gumption. I occasionally like a good challenge crop, and celery offers one of the greatest challenges. But even poorly raised celery is valuable to the home cook, so why not give it a shot?

RIGHT: The rare red heirloom celery called 'Giant Red' is indeed a giant if grown well. **OPPOSITE:** Celery demands the highest level of fertility and water but will reward growers with the largest plants. Anything less and the result will be bitter, hollow stalks and foliage best only as an herb.

VARIETIES

'Conquistador' open-pollinated (80 days)—Standard market and home variety with long stalks.

'Tango' open-pollinated (80 days)—Good new variety for home gardeners. Taller than most varieties and less fibrous. Tolerant to heat and stress.

'Redventure' open-pollinated (110 days)—Heirloom red celery with stalks that have reddish-green stems. A newer introduction bred by Frank Morton. **NOTE:** Red celery is rarely dark red, and photos are often enhanced in seed catalogs.

'Utah 52-70 R' open-pollinated (110 days)—The new improved strain of the old standard 'Utah', which is also still available, but '52-70 R' is far better, especially in home gardens.

CELERIAC

Apium graveolens var. *rapaceum*

While celery can be challenging, celeriac (also known as celery root) is not. Treated in much the same way as regular celery, celeriac requires less fertilizing and watering. Once known as "celery turnip," celeriac has many uses in the kitchen. Served either raw in salads or cooked like potatoes, it is frequently encountered in restaurants and is gradually gaining a following, although it is far from new.

Celeriac can be harvested in the autumn, then stored in damp sand in a cellar, or it can be left until the ground is nearly freezing, then dug, washed, and stored in a refrigerator drawer. Visually, celeriac is an ugly root, yet it remains a luxury market vegetable.

HOW TO GROW CELERIAC

Celeriac should be started early indoors, and it requires warmth and light. Sow seed as early as late January and cover it lightly with soil. Be patient, as seed can take as long as a month to germinate. Keep soil evenly moist and strive for a soil temperature around 60°F—any lower

OPPOSITE: Easier to grow than celery, celeriac is a long-season crop best left to those with extra space in the garden. But it's worth growing if one uses celeriac, as supermarket bulbs are inferior to homegrown, especially if consumed raw in salads for that crunch.

and the plants may bolt later in the garden. Seedlings can handle transplanting well when small, and can be moved to 3-inch pots if they grow too large. Celeriac and celery are both slow growers. They will occupy a garden bed for an entire season.

Set plants out into the garden once warm daytime temperatures are constant—5 days or more under 50°F will cause plants to flower too early. This is a common mistake that can happen when growers attempt to harden their young plants off too early. The finest celeriac comes from healthy seedlings that were set out at the proper time in late spring and spaced correctly (6 to 10 inches apart), then fed and watered properly. Don't harvest the celeriac roots until autumn.

VARIETIES

'Mars' open-pollinated (95 days)—The professional grower's choice for celeriac as it is disease-resistant and tolerant to occasional dry periods in warm, humid climates.

'Giant Prague' open-pollinated (110 days)—Heirloom variety that can grow large roots. Popular European strain.

PARSLEY

Petroselinum crispum

You can never have too much parsley in the kitchen. More often than not, a few pots of parsley are picked up from a garden center in the spring and set into the corners of a raised bed, or used in an herb container near the kitchen door. But as any cook knows, these few containers may need to be cut clean just to season a single batch of chicken stock or bone broth. In the vegetable garden, even a 6-foot row of parsley may need expansion to supply parsley-heavy dishes such as tabbouleh.

Treating parsley as a serious vegetable crop makes sense. I've often been teased when I mention that I have two 10-foot rows of parsley, but experience has taught me that I can easily go through two bunches a week with pasta dishes alone. And given that there are many superior varieties, ranging from flavorful flat-leaf to curly-leaved types, I can truly justify the space.

The most important reason to invest in raising more parsley is your health. Parsley is highly nutritious, but commercially raised parsley is also a relatively dirty chemical crop, drenched in insecticides and fungicides due to its attractiveness to pollinators. It's a caterpillar magnet, which is something I am okay with in the home garden.

SOME PARSLEY MYTHS

1. "Parsley doesn't mind cold weather, so it's okay to sow seed outdoors as soon as the soil can be worked."

It's easy to understand why so many believe that parsley is cold tolerant in the spring, because visually the plants seem to be able to handle very cold weather. The danger is that the damage happens invisibly, inside the young plant. Cold-afflicted plants will grow just fine until warm weather arrives, but then they will bolt and go to seed.

As with many biennials in the family Apiaceae, exposure to cold weather stimulates certain phytohormones in parsley. It is best started from seed indoors under warm lights set to 16 hours of daylight, then set out once the soil has warmed to 60°F.

2. "Parsley doesn't require much fertilizer."

Knowing the fertility requirements of anything you plant is essential. For parsley, a balanced feed of 5-10-5 is recommended for the first month, with granular fertilizer side-dressing at least twice during the summer. You want lush green foliage as well as strong roots, so additional phosphorus in the spring will help get plants established. A balanced feed (5-5-5) throughout the growing season will ensure that enough nitrogen is available as this is a leaf crop, and nitrogen is short-lived.

Parsley plants sold at nurseries often look healthy, but those gorgeous 4-inch pots of bushy parsley were designed to look better than they should. A perfect parsley seedling to set out into the garden should actually look a little skimpy. If you are growing from starts, choose a single plant in a single pot that is not too big. Commercial plug growers sow multiple seeds into each plug, resulting in 4-inch pots that appear bushy and healthy but are comprised of multiple plants growing too closely together. To make matters worse, there are new pot-sized varieties bred for spring sales that tend to be squat and bushy but are inferior as culinary varieties for the garden.

PARSLEY VARIETIES

There are a surprising number of parsley varieties, far beyond what most just see as flat-leaf and curly. Those are types. There are very choice named varieties available, and the best seed suppliers will list them proudly. If you are a serious cook or chef, seek out some of the new and heirloom varieties and grow an assortment. Read the descriptions carefully in seed catalogs and learn which variety meets your needs the best.

HOW TO GROW PARSLEY

Pre-soak seed for 24 hours by covering it with hot water. Drain, and sow parsley either in individual cell containers (3 or 4 seeds in a single hole ¼ inch deep) or in a seed tray. Cover seed with ¼ inch of sifted sterile soilless mix or vermiculite, which will help reduce fungus and keep the seed moist. Cover tray or cells with plastic wrap and set somewhere warm (around 80°F). Parsley can tolerate transplanting when still very young if you are pressed for space. A slight shift in temperature from day to night also aids in germination. If raising indoors under lights, this should naturally happen at night when the light timer is off. Maintain constant dampness, not allowing seed containers to dry out or get too soggy. Patience is required, as germination can take 3 weeks.

Once seedlings have emerged, a light feed every 3 weeks will help them remain strong. I fertilize biweekly with a water-soluble fertilizer slightly higher in phosphorus—a ratio close to 5-10-5 is ideal.

If raising seedlings in community pots, transplant to individual pots early. Seedlings handle transplanting fine if they have not formed their third set of leaves.

Set plants outdoors into the prepared soil (rich, moisture-retentive loam) only when temperatures have warmed in late spring, avoiding exposure to cold weather (below 45°F). Side-dress rows with 5-10-5 fertilizer every 3 weeks. As a green herb, parsley needs constant fertility to remain green and tender.

Plants are remarkably cold tolerant in the autumn, and in mild climates they will overwinter to provide additional greens the following spring before they bloom and die. Mature plants can be dug and potted to extend the harvest a bit if you have a cold greenhouse or a sun porch, but the quality will be inferior to outdoor plants.

Just as there are select fancy salts (like Himalayan pink and French Fleur de Sel), there are now new and very choice parsley varieties for connoisseurs. Why settle for generic curly or flat-leaf Italian parsley when you could have extraordinary types as tightly curled as woodland moss or as flavorful and crispy as the finest celery leaf?

Parsley seedlings must be started early. Plug trays will make transplanting individual plants easier. Keep parsley plants warm until the weather has turned mild, because exposure to temperatures lower than 50°F for even a few days can vernalize plants, resulting in plants that will bloom and thus go to seed by midsummer rather than lasting into the following year, as biennials typically would.

VARIETIES

CURLY TYPE

'Favorite' open-pollinated (75 days)—A very curly 'Paramount' type ('Paramount' was a 1936 AAS winner) with a good flavor profile that isn't too bitter. Tender, with an upright growing habit.

'Antaris' open-pollinated (75 days)—The absolute curliest parsley variety—it almost looks like a ball of moss. Hard to find as it sells out quickly, but worth seeking out.

'Darki' open-pollinated (75 days)—A curly type with a shorter growth habit and very dark leaves. Good for both containers and in the garden.

FLAT-LEAF TYPE

'Fidelio' F1 hybrid—An improved flat-leaf Italian type with resistance to downy mildew.

DILL

Anethum graveolens

Another plant with a long history dating back to the Egyptians is dill, an herb commonly associated with pickling and with Scandinavian dishes. Growing fresh dill in the garden makes sense, especially if there is a cook in the house.

Having a constant supply of fresh dill can be challenging, and like many plants in the carrot family, incorrect cultural tips can lead you to believe that dill is simply not worth the effort. Sometimes available as young plants in the spring (sold along with other herbs at garden centers), dill is never a plant you should buy as a seedling. It despises transplanting and hates any root disturbance. The good news is that, unlike parsley, dill is a rapid grower when sown directly into the garden.

CHOOSING THE RIGHT VARIETY OF DILL

Before you begin with dill, it's helpful to think about how you plan to use it in the kitchen. There are dill cultivars specifically bred for their ferny leaves that are well suited for fresh coleslaw, salads, and sprinkling onto dishes like roasted beets or salmon.

Then there are dill varieties that are best for pickling, which requires both the greens and the seeds. These are taller types with tough, woody stems and huge umbels of golden-yellow flowers that you can pick either in bloom or when they are in the seed stage, depending on the recipe. Many home chefs raise both types, and their culture is very much the same.

Regardless of how often you pick dill, it is best planted in long rows of successive plantings. Dill raised for its greens will also bloom and set seed, but most varieties are resistant to bolting. If allowed to set seed naturally and self-sow, all varieties will revert to a more vigorous type that has woodier stems and flavorful seeds. If you don't use mulch, a single planting of dill can ensure a constant supply for years to come.

RAISING DILL

Because dill seed is large, it is very easy to sow. Seed can be sown early, as soon as the ground is thawed and can be worked. Sow directly into prepared soil that has been raked smooth. Sow in rows or bands, spacing seeds 2 to 3 inches apart for seed-head varieties, or 1 inch apart for leafy varieties. With seed-head pickling varieties, thin the seedlings to 4 to 6 inches apart as these taller plants will perform better with the extra space. For a constant supply of dill, do successive plantings every 3 to 4 weeks, and don't forget to time pickling types to match your cucumber harvest.

OPPOSITE: Dill provides two harvests; the first brings flavorful, ferny foliage, and the second lovely flower umbels and fragrant seedheads—perhaps the most valuable gift dill bestows us, especially pickle-makers.

VARIETIES

BUNCHING DILL

'Hera' open-pollinated (50 days)—More uniform as a fresh green herb. The slowest to bolt; grown more as a bunching herb.

'Fernleaf' open-pollinated (60 days)—Good for containers. Slower to go to seed and a good variety for leaf production. Can be sown thicker in rows than types grown for seed heads and pickling spices.

SEED DILL

'Super Dukat' open-pollinated—Offers the best of both seeding and fern-leaf types, yet slower to bolt.

'Bouquet' open-pollinated (45 days)—Tall, old-fashioned habit. Grown for leaf and seed. Excellent for pickling, and the best for large seed heads.

ABOVE: Dill seed has a stronger and different flavor than its foliage. **LEFT:** If raising dill for pickling, choose varieties that produce strong stems and flowers rather than those intended as fresh, leafy herbs. **OPPOSITE:** Dill flowers can be picked before they produce seed, but always leave a few to mature and spread seeds around the garden.

CILANTRO
Coriandrum sativum

If you buy cilantro every time you visit the supermarket, then growing your own will not only save time and money, it will offer you a constant supply of an herb essential for so many dishes. Cilantro, like its kin, can be fussy, but in many ways, it is the easiest of the carrot family to grow, as long as you can offer it what it needs.

Cilantro success begins with variety. Some cultures use the roots, while others use the seeds and leaf. Few, however, raise garden cilantro for its seeds, which are difficult to harvest (with the exception of immature green coriander seed, used for certain dishes).

Buying cilantro plants or starts at a garden center is simply a waste of money, unless you are planning on harvesting it as soon as you arrive at home in the driveway. Cilantro is such a rapidly growing crop that it doesn't make any sense to buy a plant at any size, let alone a large one.

Failure with cilantro often comes from simple inattention to the most basic details: starting with seed directly sown (never transplanted), plenty of water, food, and soil. Most importantly, cilantro grows best in cooler weather. Cilantro seed is large, round, and easy to sow, and the plant is very fast to reach a harvestable size, yet like many of its relatives, any root disturbance or stress can cause the plants

OPPOSITE: Cilantro grows best in cooler weather, especially in autumn, when the leaves taste less soapy.

to bolt. If the soil is deficient in any nutrients, the seedlings will be stunted and turn anemic.

CHOOSING THE RIGHT VARIETY

Like parsley or dill, no two cilantro varieties are the same anymore. Its popularity has motivated plant breeders to develop varieties that can handle a bit more stress (such as growing closer together in pots for spring sales) but are rather useless if sown directly into the kitchen garden. Be sure to look for varieties that are not pictured growing in a small pot, and list traits such as slow-bolting for maximum performance.

Cilantro is more likely to bolt when daytime temperatures rise above 80°F. However, Cilantro doesn't bolt because it hates heat, it bolts because it grows faster in the hotter summer months, and because it may be stressed from a missed watering or two. Most commercial cilantro is raised in Oregon and the Pacific Northwest. Often the finest cilantro comes from later sowings in early autumn because it comes closest to the flavor of supermarket cilantro.

HOW TO GROW CILANTRO

Many suggest that cilantro should be sown thickly, but I've found that thinner sowing in the spring and late summer when temperatures are cooler will produce larger plants that seem to bolt a little later. You can also thin them when plants are still very small, and use the greens in

the kitchen. Never transplant cilantro and avoid buying plants started in pots. Most plants at the garden center are already mature and will go to seed immediately after planting in the garden.

Sow fresh cilantro seeds on a strict, continuous schedule if you need a constant supply, especially during the hottest summer months. Many market farmers continue to raise quality cilantro throughout the summer, opting to harvest plants younger and sow more often. With steady irrigation and a balanced fertilizer regimen (5-5-5), cilantro can be had throughout the growing season.

Plan ahead and order enough seed to sow at least five plantings during the season, beginning in mid-spring after all threat of frost has passed. Direct-sow 4- or 5-foot rows. Maturity is slower in cooler weather when plants are less likely to bolt, suggesting 5-week planting intervals. During the hottest months, sow seed weekly and harvest every 2½ to 3 weeks.

Harvest spring and autumn cilantro with scissors. Leave a few new leaves on the plant, or cut it in its entirety. Summer cilantro can be sown thicker and harvested sooner when they are younger plants.

In any season, water and high fertility are important, as cilantro can go anemic quickly. If sowing in raised beds or containers with a soilless potting mix, make sure the mix was not used for a previous crop, or the cilantro may grow weakly and turn yellow. Cilantro is very sensitive to environmental stress, whether from temperature extremes or from lack of nutrients or water. A fall crop sown in August is often the best crop of the season.

CILANTRO MYTHS

There seem to be as many myths about how to raise cilantro as there are for other members of the carrot family. Most are not true. For example, cutting the flower stem once a plant starts blooming will not extend its life. And don't expect five or six harvests from a row of cilantro. One or two harvests per seeded row is more realistic.

VARIETIES

'Calypso' open-pollinated (50 days plus)—Best for garden use. Slower to bolt than unnamed varieties.

'Santo' open-pollinated (50 days plus)—Slow-bolting variety better for containers as it is not as large as other varieties. Can be used for seed production as well (coriander seed).

'Cruiser' open-pollinated (50 days plus)—Really the new standard as it grows tighter (yet still tall) and is slower to bolt than both 'Santo' and 'Calypso'. A premium market or bunching variety that produces taller plants that are known to be slower to bolt.

'Santo Monogerm' open-pollinated (50 days plus)—Because cilantro seeds are botanically fruits (with multiple seeds inside), 'Santo Monogerm' seeds have been split so that growers can sow individual plants more precisely. Great for home gardeners who want to grow larger cilantro plants by sowing them spaced. Also good for growing cilantro roots (used in many Asian dishes) as the roots will grow larger.

OPPOSITE: If cilantro does bloom, allow some to set seed; its seed is another spice—coriander—and green coriander seed is a delicacy rarely offered in stores. **ABOVE:** Cilantro will bolt and go to seed in hot weather.

7

BEANS, PEAS, AND OKRA

Along with the vegetables that changed world civilizations after the discovery of America—potatoes, corn, and the solanums like tomatoes and peppers—are beans. To be precise, those within the genus *Phaseolus*—New World beans that changed the diet of many global cultures. It's hard to imagine a world without beans today, especially given their popularity in so many regional cuisines.

Beans (and other legumes within Fabaceae) are particularly fascinating to scientists due to their ability to absorb nitrogen gasses through specially developed root nodules, which creates an environment that attracts nitrifying bacteria.

This ability to absorb nitrogen is good not only for the beans, but also for those who consume them. Their talent for nitrogen absorption allows bean plants to assemble amino acids into the proteins essential in human dietary needs. Therefore, beans have historically aided in famine relief and are an essential part of many cuisines.

Broadly, we can divide beans into two groups: dried and fresh. The dried seeds are a familiar winter vegetable—jarred and stored, they are reconstituted in water, added to soups, stews, and chilies, and even pureed, as in refried beans.

Fresh beans are a little more complex, but most gardeners usually choose to grow the most common beans—green beans or yellow wax beans (the "wax" name is often used for any yellow-podded bean, as seventeenth-century farmers believed they looked as if made of beeswax). These are the beans we often see sold in cans at the supermarket, frozen in poly bags, or eaten at holiday dinners.

However, if you limit yourself to only green and wax beans in your vegetable garden, an entire universe of beans remains to be discovered. Many of the lesser-known varieties have extraordinary characteristics and are rarely offered in stores as fresh produce.

BROAD (FAVA) BEANS
Vicia faba

Things are looking brighter for the oft-maligned "horse bean"—a name coined by eighteenth-century American farmers who felt fava beans were too big and worthy only for animal feed. Today, thanks to a more informed audience consisting of obsessed foodies, adventurous small farmers, and curious gardeners, the fava bean is discovering a new fan base that can appreciate this tender and delicious legume.

Planting broad beans on a cold autumn day is a chore any allotment gardener in the United Kingdom is familiar with. British gardeners often post about this ritual on social media and gardening blogs. Most nongardeners outside of the Middle East and Britain will most likely associate fava beans with the film *The Silence of the Lambs*. That's because they have never tasted a broad bean, let alone seen a pod at the market or growing in a garden. These beans have simply been off the radar.

Fava beans are ancient. Archaeologists have found dried beans in Egyptian tombs and even artwork depicting the pods much earlier in the Middle East, but their spread to the rest of the world hasn't been as noteworthy. Aside from their popularity in England and throughout the Mediterranean, elsewhere this bean has remained

practically a novelty. Broad beans are not new in the United States or Canada. Even though they are difficult to find fresh at markets, there was a time when many home gardeners grew them. North American seed suppliers in the mid-1800s listed as many as 30 cultivars and often called them simply "English beans."

It's unfortunate that fava beans never established themselves as a major crop in North America. Had they been grown in quantity, they could have filled a gap between late winter forced crops and summer crops. Although the earliest colonists were familiar with fava beans from growing them in England, the Industrial Revolution may have pushed them into obsolescence when rail travel suddenly allowed nationwide shipment of Californian and southern crops year-round.

HOW TO GROW FAVA BEANS

Raising your own fava beans is the best, if not the only, option if you want to enjoy this spring treat. Although they look like lima beans, especially when dried, it's the fresh bean that the home gardener should cherish. The large bean seeds are not dry and mealy, but rather sweet and bright green like an early spring pea. When consumed fresh they are delightful, with the benefit of size— each fresh bean seed is about equal to a heaping teaspoon of shelled green sweet peas.

Broad beans like cold weather and can be sown as soon as the ground can be worked. In

OPPOSITE: Broad beans or fava beans enjoy long, cool summers and can be prolific in northern gardens if sown early, before the weather becomes hot and humid.

colder climates you may want to try starting some in individual pots. Seedlings must be transplanted very carefully and with no root disturbance. Transplanting broad beans may not be ideal, but where spring weather is unpredictable and summer heat and humidity risks arriving too early, getting pre-started plants into the cold soil as early as possible may mean the difference between a nice harvest and none.

In the United Kingdom and in mild-winter areas like the coastal Pacific Northwest, broad beans are sown in autumn so they can appreciate the long, cool, damp winter. They are indeed a winter crop in these climates, but elsewhere, if you can get the timing right on the calendar, fresh beans make for a terrific early spring crop.

Direct-sowing seed outdoors is the optimum method for raising broad beans. In much of USDA Zones 4 to 6, seed can be sown in the open soil during mild winters with little fear of damage. Late February through mid-April you can set seeds 2 to 3 inches apart and 2 inches deep directly into the cold soil. Light snow will not hurt even young seedlings (provided they have been exposed to cold weather their entire young lives), but a light covering of fleece or a row cover can be used if serious snow threatens. If transplanting pre-started plants, do so only after they have been hardened off outdoors for a week or so. Growth may be slow for the first few weeks, but be assured that roots are growing down. Once the weather begins to warm to 50°F or 60°F, growth will quicken.

Broad beans are not vines like pole beans, but they are not bush beans either. Rather, they grow more like okra, producing a single stem and usually growing straight up. Blossoms will form quickly, followed by large seed pods so heavy they can cause plants to tip over. Staking will help prevent this. A simple method is to set a row of tomato stakes on either side of the bean plants, then wrap twine around each stake and run the line down each side of the row to box the towering plants in.

Moisture is essential throughout the growing season. If your area is prone to early dry periods, keep a hose handy. Be certain to water plants well as they are taprooted and prefer a deep watering. As plants begin to flower and form pods, you can speed things along by pinching off the central growing point (3 to 4 inches off the top of the plant)—this will help the plant focus not on new growth, but on maturing pods. This will also help with any aphid problems, because aphids enjoy broad beans, and the growing point is their favorite part of the plant.

PESTS AND PROBLEMS

Broad beans have their share of pests and diseases. Aphids on the new growth are to be expected, but rarely interfere with pod formation. Large outbreaks of aphids can be easily controlled through organic methods and by pinching off the tender growing tips once pods begin to mature.

A host of other diseases can plague broad beans, mostly bacterial and fungal diseases brought on by extended warm weather and increased humidity. Bacterial and fungal diseases are identified by brown or black spots and lesions on the foliage and on the pods. While many growers will experience these spots, most outbreaks in the home garden don't affect the pods and will be gone before things become more serious. If the entire plant wilts, remove it and destroy it (don't compost it). Because the broad bean season is short, ignore the occasional collapse of a plant or two. Most bacterial problems affect big commercial farmers, who may need to turn to more aggressive methods to control the infection of a large crop.

HARVESTING BROAD BEANS

As the pods mature, they will begin to droop from the weight of the large beans inside. Cut pods off with scissors rather than trying to pull them off—the stems are tough and you can tear the entire plant. Shelling the beans is a relatively pleasurable task and goes quickly—

you can easily clean a bucket of pods in a half-hour. There is an additional step though: the seeds of broad beans have a tough outer skin that must be removed before you eat them (so popping one into your mouth while still out in the garden isn't a good idea). To remove the outer casing, the beans must be blanched for about a minute in boiling water, then immediately plunged into ice water to stop them from cooking. This process will loosen up the outer layer, and with a slight squeeze the green, fleshy bean will pop out. Then they can be frozen or used in any recipe.

Broad beans pair well with other spring vegetables like fresh asparagus. They are productive and tend to all come to maturity at once, so you can seem overwhelmed with beans for a while. Try freezing the extras for a winter treat you can look forward to.

VARIETIES

'Windsor' open-pollinated (75 days)—This heirloom is the standard classic variety still favored by many growers. Pods are 6 inches long and held horizontally.

'Vroma' open-pollinated (75 days)—Improved, heat-tolerant type less likely to be blown over in the wind. 7-inch pods.

'Masterpiece' open-pollinated (80 days)—The standard English variety with large pods and tall plants often over 3 feet tall. RHS award winner.

'Extra Precoce a Grano Violetto' heirloom (80 days)—Old variety with purple pods and beans favored in some parts of northern Italy.

'Windsor' broad bean (or fava bean).

COMMON BEANS
Phaseolus sp.

What most of us know as common beans—the string beans and shell beans—are considered New World beans. Native to South America, they were already grown by indigenous people in parts of North America by the time the earliest colonists began to arrive.

A BRIEF HISTORY OF THE COMMON BEAN

When "American beans" arrived in Europe in the late 1400s, entire diets were changed. Rapidly, the bean became popular in Spain, Portugal, and Italy, where it transformed soups and dishes in its dried form. It was the French who transformed the dried New World bean into what we know today— a podded bean. While countries in southern Europe expanded on the use of dried beans, further north, gardeners were discovering an even more useful way to eat them—consuming them as immature pods.

Beans have come a long way from the tough-podded shell beans of pre-Columbian times. In the early 1800s, seeds for a variety known as 'Flageolet Vert' (named after an ancient French woodwind instrument that is long and thin) became all the rage near Paris. The flageolet pods were harvested when the seed inside was still fresh, and this variety became incredibly popular throughout Europe as a dried shell bean

OPPOSITE: 'Velour' is a fancy French filet or Haricot vert bean best picked while the pods are very thin and stringless. They turn green once cooked.

(because it held its green color) and served fresh as well. In fact, the flageolet became so popular that dwarf varieties were developed, including red-, black-, and white-seeded varieties. In France, most were first bred for greenhouse-forcing to provide fresh beans during the colder months. As these varieties reached North America, they were known as 'French Forcing Flageolet' and were available in the mid-nineteenth century in green, purple, and yellow wax varieties.

In the nineteenth century, all string beans had strings—tough fibers on each end of the pod that had to be removed. Most thought this string was a necessary part of the bean functionally. Calvin Keeney of Leroy, New York—a.k.a. the "string-bean man"—was the breeder of the first stringless string bean: 'Stringless Refugee Wax', introduced in 1884. Mr. Keeney is indeed the father of most modern string beans, as he introduced many parents of the stringless varieties we grow today.

GROWING BUSH BEANS

Aside from watering and weeding, beans are relatively low-maintenance in most gardens. They relish warm weather and soils, so prefer to be sown after any threat of frost, when the soil has warmed to over 70°F. They can be started early in individual cell packs, but given their dislike of root disturbance, and the number of plants needed to get a respectable crop, it's best to sow directly into the ground.

Most bean varieties are bred for commercial requirements, such as uniform sizes for mechanical picking or to fit neatly in a can, but at home some exceptional varieties are actually pole beans. Try 'Fortex' (left), a bean with 10-inch straight pods; 'Anellino Giallo' (center), an heirloom with a twisted shrimplike shape; or the yellow pods of 'Meraviglia di Venezia' or 'Miracle of Venice' (right), a variety with rich flavor and productive vines.

Bush or dwarf types can be planted close together—one method is to trench the seeds thickly, as when sowing peas. Dig an 8-inch-wide trench and broadcast the seeds into it heavily, with some seeds even touching. This method, introduced in the 1970s on the PBS show *Crockett's Victory Garden*, proves successful for many northern gardeners. Dusting the seeds first with legume inoculant is recommended, especially for thicker sowing. Thickly sown bands should be spaced at least 36 inches apart, as the multitude of plants can overwhelm more space than you'd think. No need to thin seedlings if the soil is rich. Beans can grow closely.

The more traditional way to sow beans is to set eight seeds per foot at 1 inch deep. Germination can be slow if the weather is cold, but if the soil is warm and moist, seeds will emerge within 6 days. Black-seeded or purple-podded varieties tolerate cool soil conditions better than other types.

Bush beans mature nearly all at the same time (with perhaps a smaller second harvest), so be prepared for a rush of beans, as well as some surplus to share

or preserve. Experienced gardeners know that beans always seem to arrive in the kitchen in great quantity on the hottest day of the year. If you plan on canning or freezing part of your crop, it's wise to have the materials ready a few weeks in advance.

GROWING POLE BEANS

Pole beans appear to have fallen out of favor with some gardeners, but they do offer some practical benefits—especially to those with limited space or those who don't want to break their backs when picking beans. They offer a longer fruiting season than bush beans as well, with smaller beans maturing at the top of the plant after the bottom ones are harvested. Some may think pole beans are troublesome because they are vines, but in actuality, few plants are as easy to grow. The use of specially designed pole-bean towers is beneficial. Found in garden supply catalogs, the towers look like extra-tall tomato towers, but are constructed from heavy-gauge wire. These prefabricated towers make growing pole beans easy, and the towers can be used in another season for other vining crops like cucumbers, lima beans, or Malabar spinach. Although there is no denying that a traditional teepee structure made from bamboo or branches makes an attractive garden statement, they are not ideal for growing pole beans. Like all vines, pole beans want to sprawl more than these structures will allow.

GROWING DRIED BEANS

Dried beans are usually pole beans, although a few are bush beans. While it's true that any bean could be considered a dry bean, some varieties are better suited for drying. Few gardeners seem to grow dried beans anymore,

yet not only are they easy—you can sow a few bean towers in a far corner of the garden and forget about them until fall—they are also fun to shell. Kids love discovering the various types and admiring their unusual colors.

Harvest bean pods in the autumn as they begin to dry and fade on the plants. This may take a few rounds in the garden with scissors. Try to keep a bowl for each variety. As pods dry further inside a warm, dry house, some will split. Dry the pods on an uncovered cookie sheet or any flat surface for 2 to 4 weeks, or until the pods are paper-dry and the beans inside are hard and shiny. There are hundreds of dried bean varieties, and

These heirloom 'Eye of the Tiger' beans date back to 1839 and can be harvested as a snap bean when young, or as a shiny black bean once dried on the vine.

VARIETIES

BUSH GREEN BEANS

'Provider' open-pollinated (50 days)—The standard heirloom against which all green beans are measured. Still as good as ever.

'Rocdor' open-pollinated (55 days)—Deep yellow, pencil-thin pods.

PURPLE POD BEANS

'Amethyst' open-pollinated (56 days)—Uniform dark-purple pods that will turn green when cooked but are lovely on a raw vegetable tray.

POLE BEANS

'Fortex' open-pollinated (60 days)—A vigorous green bean with 9-inch pods that will need a bean tower. It produces long pods that are uniform and high-yielding.

'Monte Gusto' open-pollinated (58 days)—Yellow pole bean with 7- to 8-inch pods.

'Meraviglia di Venezia' open-pollinated (58 days)—'Marvel of Venice'—a classic flat-podded yellow 'Roma' type that is high-yielding and delicious.

'Anellino' open-pollinated (57 days)—Heirloom Italian "shrimp-shaped" beans that almost grow into little rings. Hard to find in the United States. Available in green or yellow varieties.

DRIED SHELL BEANS

'Cannellino' open-pollinated (55 days)—White cannellini beans great for soups or puree.

'Cherokee Trail of Tears' heirloom (75 days)—Small black beans; highly sought-after heirloom.

'Jacob's Cattle' heirloom (75 days)—White and maroon speckled bean.

'Ojo de Cabra' heirloom (80 days)—'Eye of the Goat' bean, a landrace type from Baja, Mexico.

'Ojo de Tigre' heirloom (80 days)—Old Mexican golden-colored bean with dark stripes.

'Rio Zape' heirloom (95 days)—Mexican mauve and brown bean. Nominated for Slow Food USA's "Ark of Taste."

while some varieties have particular uses, all can be used interchangeably in everything from baked beans to the earthiest of French soups.

Plant a few towers of various types at a far end of your vegetable garden. Remember that they will need a long season, as the vines will need to remain in place until the pods are mature and dry. If a hard frost threatens, pick all the pods and allow them to ripen indoors. The beans will still dry, but at a different stage of maturity, which will only affect the color.

OPPOSITE: Dried beans freshly picked after a light frost has killed the foliage are allowed to dry before shelling. From left to right: 'Tigre', 'Monachelle Di Trevio', 'Cherokee Trail of Tears' black bean, 'Yellow Tiger's Eye' ('Ojo de Tigre'), and pink 'Tigre'.

PEAS
Pisum sativum

While peas made their way to the New World with the very first colonists, their history in gardens reaches as far back as antiquity. Researchers cannot agree on exactly where peas were domesticated (central Asia most likely, or perhaps India), but most can agree on when—around the same time that wheat and barley were domesticated. Thus, peas are indeed one of the most ancient of all domesticated crops.

We presume that peas were popular because of their flavor, but the truth is that the peas we enjoy today are nothing at all like the dried peas that nourished families in the Middle Ages.

Throughout much of history, peas were grown as a dry seed for winter storage, then reconstituted in soups and stews. Pease porridge was so common throughout Europe and early America that it's been documented that early Americans often ate peas three times a day. While a bowl of modern split-pea soup has its merits, few of us would want to eat it every day.

It wasn't until the 1700s that green peas were shelled from their tough pods and eaten fresh. By the Victorian era, peas were so cherished that seed catalogs often featured them on the first few pages, as well as on the cover. Many were named

after the technological trends of the Industrial Revolution era. Thus, popular pea varieties were introduced with names like 'Phonograph', 'Telegraph', and 'Telephone', honoring the amazing inventions of the early 1880s.

CULTURE

Peas require some planning from the home gardener. As a cool-weather crop, you need to sow peas very early in the spring or even in late winter. Do this as soon as possible, as long as the soil is not frozen or muddy.

Not particularly fussy about soil nutrition, peas are sensitive to soil pH, preferring soils that are slightly more alkaline than acidic. If you have performed a soil test, the ideal range is between 6.0 and 7.5. Adjust soil pH with ground dolomitic limestone applied and dug-in deeply the previous autumn. This will ensure that the lime is well distributed and the necessary chemistry has begun, and it will help reduce soil disturbance at planting time.

If your soil is rich with organic matter (compost, peat), it should drain quickly in late winter, and digging a trench for pea seed should be easy. Planting pea seed is often the first activity many of us do in the garden.

When choosing which type of pea to plant, it may be helpful to know that edible-podded types such as snap peas or snow peas will offer a greater yield with less waste per square foot, if only because you eat the pod as well. Shelling peas ups

OPPOSITE: Plant peas thickly in long rows to maximize yields. Choose new, shorter-growing varieties to eliminate the need for tall trellising, but a bit of chicken wire will help.

VARIETIES

SHELLING PEAS

'Sienna' open-pollinated (55 days)—Midseason shell pea with 28-inch vines that can either be staked or allowed to tumble. High-yielding vines with 8 to 9 peas per pod.

'Maxigolt' open-pollinated (62 days)—Late pea that is short-growing and often doesn't need to be staked if sown thickly (but best if allowed to climb on wire). Only 24 inches tall with 3½-inch pods. Excellent disease resistance.

'Penelope' open-pollinated (59 days)—Tall 36-inch vines producing high-quality ½-inch pea pods with eight to nine peas. One of the most disease-resistant varieties, including resistance to Fusarium, powdery mildew, and pea mosaic virus.

SNOW PEAS

'Oregon Giant' open-pollinated (60 days)—Tall vines up to 32 inches with high yields of large, flat snow pea pods. Very disease-resistant.

'Royal Snow' open-pollinated (61 days)—Dark-purple pods great for serving raw with dips, they lose color when cooked, even turning brownish.

'Golden Sweet' open-pollinated (61 days)—Novelty yellow snow pea that looks great in raw dishes along with 'Royal Snow'. Has beautiful purple flowers.

SNAP PEAS

'Super Sugar Snap' open-pollinated (60 days)—Very tall vines up to 5 feet that will need staking. Highly productive and useful—you can eat the entire shell and the pod.

'Sugar Sprint' open-pollinated (58 days)—Very short vining form with 2-foot vines that don't need staking. 3-inch pods with fewer strings than the old variety 'Sugar Ann', which it replaces.

'Penelope' produces uniform, long pods with eight to nine peas in each one.

your labor demand and creates considerably more waste. A 20-foot row of shelling peas may yield a peck and a half of pods which, once shelled, will average only a quart and a half of green peas. Home gardeners with small raised beds may have greater success with snap peas or snow peas, which can offer more sizable harvests. Nevertheless, don't be discouraged if you're considering raising shelling peas. If you want enough shelled peas to eat and to freeze for a few luxurious meals in the winter, a couple of 40-foot rows should get you there.

HOW TO GROW PEAS

Don't be afraid to sow seed thickly. Many older gardening guides advise you to sow individual pea seeds 1 to 4 inches apart. This may be a fine distance for a commercial farmer with a seed-distributing device, but it is skimpy sowing for a home garden. A thickly sown band—one that is 3 to 6 inches wide—can contain 15 to 20 seeds per foot, with some seeds nearly touching. This results in a higher yield for the home gardener. Thus, you should order pea seed in quantities no smaller than ¼ pound, which will cover an 8-foot-long row sown thickly.

Once seeds are sown, cover them with an inch of soil and water well. At this time, something for the pea vine to climb up should be added. While newer varieties are often touted as being bush types, all peas are vines, and even a 30-inch-tall variety will tumble onto the ground without the proper support. Adding stakes along with wire or netting at planting time before the seed germinates is the safest way to trellis peas. Chicken wire is preferred for most varieties. The wire can be stapled or attached with strings to wooden tomato stakes or even branches. Constructing bamboo teepees is not recommended as peas will be difficult to pick and yields will be lower due to wasted space.

Just after plants bloom, keep an eye out for pod formation. It can happen quickly, seemingly overnight. Bear in mind that shelling peas is a very labor-intensive, time-consuming task. Also, ripe peas cannot wait for a time that is convenient for you. They must be picked and shelled, then frozen or eaten almost immediately, and rarely will they time it for a sunny Saturday afternoon.

LIMA BEAN (BUTTER BEAN)

Phaseolus lunatus

Lima beans are often overlooked by home gardeners, especially in cold climates, where their long growing season keeps them off most gardeners' must-grow lists. But with a little forethought, this classic southern vegetable can be enjoyed by gardeners even in cold climates. The trick to success with this large bean is simple—choose short-season varieties, and start early.

Choose lima bean varieties recommended for your area. Cold-climate gardeners should choose varieties that require 85 days or less to mature. Standard limas do best with a long, hot summer—they need at least 90 to 100 days of weather well above 75°F to mature.

HOW TO GROW LIMA BEANS

Starting seed early in summer in cell containers is an easy way to jump-start the season. While southern gardeners may frown on it, for northern gardeners, there is no getting around the time required for mature pods. Sow the large seeds in individual 3-inch pots, as roots will need space. Be sure to maintain a soil temperature above 65°F. Plan to start lima seeds 4 to 5 weeks back from your frost-free date.

Transplant seedlings outdoors when the air temperature warms to 80°F during the day and

OPPOSITE: Fresh, green lima beans are a seasonal treat worth growing even in cooler climates, but they require a head start.

65°F at night. By this time, the plants will have formed runners. It's fine to pinch off growth if they become unruly—the plants will form new stems. If raised in cell packs or individual pots, plants will transplant easily without root damage—just be careful not to disturb the soil on the rootball.

In a prepared bed, place the young plants somewhat closely together in a row. You will need to provide something for them to climb up—limas grow rampantly when established and can even outrun a common pole bean. You will need a sturdy trellis system or a mesh structure. Stakes and mesh should be at least 6 to 8 feet tall.

Keep lima bean plants well watered and fertilized all summer long. By late July, flower buds will begin to form, and while pods start off small, they will need a month or more to mature before they are ready for picking. Lima bean flowers are smaller than most bean varieties, but just as beautiful. Small pods will form after the bees have pollinated the flowers. Within 3 weeks, hard seed pods will become obvious on the vines.

HARVESTING LIMA BEANS

Determining when lima beans should be picked can be very tricky. Pods that look mature may not have lima beans formed inside yet, while others may have seeds that are too mature and woody. Break a few pods open to see if the seeds have formed yet.

Green, fresh limas are like fresh peas for eating out of hand. While many will joke about miserable lima beans served for dinner during their childhood, the truth is that fresh lima beans are amazing—simply served with butter and salt they are a treat worth waiting for every year.

Of course, you can also dry the beans, but you may not have enough to make it worth the bother. At best, you may want to freeze some for a couple of meals. If you do happen to plant a 100-foot row and end up with too many to deal with, they can be dried.

Also, at the end of the season, any remaining pods can be allowed to dry on the vines, and the seeds harvested for winter dishes. Dry the large, pale seeds gently in the sun or on a table indoors, and then store in a jar in a cool, dry place. Dried limas can be soaked overnight and then prepared as fresh beans or added to winter soups and stews, but fair warning—these may remind you of those mealy, large limas of your youth.

ALL: 'Fordhook 242' beans.

VARIETIES

'Fordhook 242' heirloom (85 days)—An old standard and an AAS winner from 1945. It is still the go-to lima for home growers, especially in cold climates.

'Jackson Wonder' heirloom (103 days)—A speckled lima with buff and chestnut-brown beans. Best for drying. The seeds are lovely and could almost be used as jewelry.

'King of the Garden' heirloom (110 days)—A big plant with 8-inch pods, this heirloom produces large seeds. It is best grown only in warm climates, as it needs long, hot summer weather to grow to its full potential.

COWPEAS

Vigna unguiculata

One of the most important crops in the African diet due to their high protein content, cowpeas (also known as black-eyed peas or crowder peas because their peas are so closely packed in their seedpods) are finally getting their due in the Western world.

The species *Vigna unguiculata* is organized into three cultivar groups. The Unguiculata group includes the cowpeas, with the black-eyed pea being by far the most common. The Sesquipedalis group includes the Chinese yard-long beans. The last group is called the Biflora group and includes lesser-known peas like sow-peas.

Cowpeas thrive in poor, dry soils and in areas with low rainfall. Not surprisingly then, cowpeas have deep taproots—some as much as 5 to 8 feet long. In home vegetable gardens, cowpeas offer high yields with minimal work. The plants are quick-growing, and some could even be considered attractive. A small lot could be converted to cowpeas and yield enough peas to feed a family for an entire winter.

There are four subspecies with varying traits, such as climbing varieties and bush varieties. There are also many heirlooms available, primarily from the American South, where the crowder pea is considered soul food. Now that they are showing up in northern US markets as a dried pea, it won't be long before more home gardeners want to try their own.

HOW TO GROW COWPEAS

Most anyone can grow this southern favorite, easily direct-sown in warm climates once the soil has warmed. A legume inoculant will help if sowing into soil where plants have never been raised before. In colder climates, start plants early: 4 to 6 weeks before last frost date. Sow two or three seeds into a 3-inch pot and cut all but two plants when they emerge to minimize root disturbance. Use conventional black greenhouse trays that hold fifteen 3-inch pots—three trays can plant an entire bed.

Plant seedlings with their first true leaves out only when the weather has fully warmed, with nighttime temperatures that stay above 65°F. Lean soils are fine. It's true that cowpeas can tolerate drought, but they'll produce best with average irrigation of 1 inch per week. Choose bush varieties if you don't want to trellis the vines. Even a row of dwarf plants can look attractive in the garden, especially if you're growing red-podded varieties.

OPPOSITE: Cowpeas have great diversity. Starting at top right: 'Hog Brains', an heirloom from Arkansas; 'Old Timer', a bush variety with speckles; 'White Whippoorwill', a southern heirloom; 'Red Heirloom'; 'Mitchell Family Cream', an heirloom from Tennessee; 'California Blackeye', so old that Thomas Jefferson grew it; 'Holstein', a rare black and white pea; in the center, 'Pigott Family Heirloom' from Washington Parish in Louisiana; in the pod, 'Clay', a Civil War staple in the South.

Cowpea varieties are as pretty as jewels, with dozens of heirloom varieties often handed down among families.

HOW TO HARVEST COWPEAS

Soon after flowering in midsummer, the pods will begin to form. While young pods could be eaten much like green beans, most black-eyed pea fans wait for the first crop of immature green peas, which are a special summer treat. Pick pods that are full, and shell the firm but still-green peas.

Most growers dry cowpeas. Allow the pods to fully mature, which may mean leaving them on the plants until early autumn. Before frost threatens, as the foliage begins to yellow, pull plants and hang them upside down to dry. Remove pods carefully if they are dry and brown, as they can split and you can lose the peas. It's fun to shell the pods, which easily split when twisted.

Because so few people raise cowpeas today, be prepared with answers when garden visitors ask what those beautiful plants are.

VARIETIES

'California Blackeye No. 5' open-pollinated (80 days)—Classic black-eyed pea with 6- to 8-inch pods for either fresh or dried use. Vining variety.

'Charm' open-pollinated (85 days)—Red-podded bush variety producing large white peas with purple eyes. High producer.

'Whippoorwill' heirloom (80 days)—Jefferson grew 'Whippoorwill' at Monticello. Produces loads of 8-inch pods containing light-brown peas with dark, chestnut-colored speckles. Primarily a dry pea. Vining.

'Clay' heirloom (75 days)—Rare pea from the Civil War era. Small peas are considered choice. Best for specialty uses and historic gardens due to low yields.

'Purple Hull Pinkeye' heirloom (80 days)—A beautiful green and purple blush covers each pod. Seeds are pale green with a purple eye. Climbing.

LEFT: 'Clay' produces thin pods with small peas that could be picked while still green and used like a green bean or allowed to dry.
RIGHT: 'Whippoorwill' drying on the vine for use as peas.

YARD-LONG BEANS

Vigna unguiculata subsp. *sesquipedalis*

Asian yard-long beans (sometimes called asparagus beans or noodle beans) have long been featured in seed catalogs in the West, but largely as a novelty vegetable. That all seems to be changing as foodies discover the fine qualities of these curiously long vegetables. Yard-long beans are becoming popular, and farmers' markets and CSAs have begun to include them. Long appreciated by the Chinese, yard-long beans are hardly as long as their name might suggest—more like half a yard, at best. Crisp, unbelievably tender, and stringless, it's no wonder that home chefs today are turning to yard-long beans

Although they appear to be simply extra-long, curly versions of common beans, they are actually of a completely different genus, so expect some differences. They are more closely related to cowpeas than to string beans, but their culture is somewhat the same—except that yard-long beans have a slightly longer season. Their benefits in the home garden are many as, like all climbing beans, they are great space-savers. They are also highly productive.

While similar in flavor to green beans, their texture is crispier when cooked. Store-bought yard-longs can be bitter, while those fresh from the garden are sweeter and virtually identical in flavor to common green beans. There are red varieties as well, which turn green when cooked but have a similar flavor.

HOW TO GROW YARD-LONG BEANS

Yard-long beans like long, hot, humid summers, but they also like areas where summers are brief but sweltering. Seeds should be started early, either indoors under lights or outside in small pots to sit out in the sun on warm days then be brought indoors when cool weather revisits.

Starting seeds in mid-June will result in crops by mid-August. Provide netting or a 6-foot-tall bean tower for the rampant vines to grow on, as they can take over a garden once the weather becomes hot.

VARIETIES

'Red Noodle' open-pollinated (90 days)—A long, reddish-purple bean that grows well even in cold climates if started early in warmth. Productive.

'Gita' open-pollinated (90 days)—An all-green yard-long bean that is day-neutral, so it can be planted earlier in warm climates.

'Liana' open-pollinated (55 days)—An early yard-long bean that is day-neutral. Ideal for earlier crops in southern gardens or as a greenhouse crop.

OPPOSITE: Yard-long or Asian noodle beans are a delight to grow for both kids and adults. Homegrown pods are sweet and delicious versus store-bought, which often are bitter and tough. They've become one of our favorite vegetables, as they are even more productive than green beans.

EDAMAME (SOYBEANS)
Glycine max

Arguably one of the most important agricultural crops on the planet, the soybean does have its place in the home garden. Just ask anyone who enjoys edamame, which is really the only reason to consider growing soybeans at home. Botanically, edamame and soybeans are exactly the same plant, and while there are some varieties that are better for steaming, others are better as a dried bean. Many organic seed catalogs list soybeans now as edamame. Be sure to read descriptions regarding height, as some varieties can grow to 5 feet tall (but most top out at 24 inches).

Edamame is a Japanese dish of immature soybean pods that have been boiled in salted water (5 percent salt) and served whole. Guests at Japanese restaurants can peel them open or squeeze the pods, popping the tender beans into their mouths. They have become so popular that frozen edamame pods are now commonplace in the freezer aisle at supermarkets around the world, along with shelled frozen edamame.

HOW TO GROW EDAMAME

Seed can be started once the soil warms to at least 65°F. Soybeans detest cool soils, which may dictate planting in mid-June in cold climates, but certainly earlier in warm climates. Plants can be started a few weeks earlier in 3-inch pots with a sterile soilless mix. A sunny greenhouse or glassed-in porch provides a good environment for starting.

HOW TO HARVEST EDAMAME

Pods will form by midsummer, and should be picked just as the pods begin to fill. Some varieties won't fill every pod, so a few test-pods will need to be sacrificed. Depending on the variety, the entire plant can be pulled as pods mature and hung to dry, or the beans can be harvested slightly earlier for green edamame for steaming.

VARIETIES

'Tankuro' open-pollinated (75 days)—A standard Japanese variety that can be harvested young as green edamame or allowed to dry for traditional kuromame. Dried beans are black.

'Tohya' open-pollinated (78 days)—Great variety for home gardens as it is only 2 feet tall. Pods are plump with three seeds each. Best harvested by pulling the entire plant and then removing the leaves if refrigerating for later or selling at a farm stand.

'Lanco' heirloom (90 days)—A good choice for dried beans. Harvest the entire plant just as the tops begin to yellow. For edamame, hand-pick pods when they are at the proper size.

OPPOSITE: Growing what is arguably the biggest monoculture crop on the planet (soybeans) in the home garden may not seem feasible, but if you enjoy fresh edamame at Japanese restaurants, this plant will change your life.

OKRA
Abelmoschus esculentus

Okra has a direct relationship with Africa, its origin country. It's one of the few vegetables that was not present in Europe until the late nineteenth century. Even now, it plays such a minor role in European cuisine that it is difficult to find outside of areas where it grows well—it is a tropical plant that demands hot, humid weather and a long, sunny growing season.

Okra is beloved by many today, but it does garner a mixed bag of "love it or hate it" comments. It's more palatable to most people either fried or pickled. Its common use as a thickener in stews and soups creates a slimy texture that is both its signature and its most objectionable quality, depending on who you ask.

Horticulturally, few would deny the beauty of the okra plant, especially its flower. It shares the same genus as cotton and is closely related to hibiscus. It's one of the few vegetables that could successfully be included in a perennial border. While the most common variety has a pale-green pod, a quick review of good seed catalogs will reveal that you can find it in a rainbow of pod colors, accentuating its value as a garden ornamental. A collection of different okra varieties can make a spectacular display on a deck or terrace. Be sure to stake plants with bamboo canes that are deeply set and at least 4 feet tall. Depending on the variety, most plants will top out at 4 feet, but in warmer climates some okra varieties can grow over 5 feet tall.

Native to warm climates, okra thrives in the southern United States and the Caribbean, where it is an essential ingredient of many regional dishes, from Cajun gumbos to southern classics.

RAISING OKRA OUTSIDE OF ITS RANGE
Cold-climate gardeners and foodies crave okra in the summer, yet few supermarkets carry good okra, as it is best when freshly picked. For this reason, okra remains a treat most enjoyed by gardeners who raise their own. This can be accomplished in cooler climates, thanks in part to the popularity of the seed-saver movement and heirloom crops. A broader selection of okra includes new varieties that perform well outside of the warmer regions of the planet.

In addition to more cold-hardy varieties, many gardeners rely on containers for growing okra. A large container (12 inches in diameter or larger) is best, especially when filled with a soilless potting mix and limited to one plant per container. But no matter how it's planted, okra makes a beautiful ornamental, especially when it blooms—watch closely for the blossoms since they tend to open for just a brief time in the morning.

RAISING FROM SEED
In colder climates, start okra seed indoors 4 to 5 weeks before the last frost date. Sow two or three large pea-like seeds into individual 3-inch

pots, cells, or plug trays. Keep the soil very warm (85°F to 90°F); this normally requires a heating mat. Okra enjoys warmth from germination until harvest. When seedlings emerge, cut the two weakest seedlings with scissors, leaving only the strongest (do not transplant seedlings as root disturbance will stunt the plants; it's better to sow a couple seeds in a pot and leave them to grow).

Keep seedlings growing indoors until the weather is warm, and set out into the garden at a distance of 18 to 24 inches. It may not seem like it at first, but okra plants can grow large, especially in warmer climates. If using containers as the final site, transplant one plant into each large pot, taking great care not to disturb the rootball. Outdoors, a floating row cover will speed recovery and encourage quick growth, as it will keep the plants warm on unexpected chilly nights in early summer. It can be removed once the weather has fully warmed, with night-time temperatures above 65°F.

Okra isn't fussy about soils and can grow well in clay or lean soils. A single feed in early spring with a balanced fertilizer is all that is necessary. If you have rich soil, even this may not be needed. In fact, okra often bears better in poor soil.

VARIETIES

'Clemson Spineless' open-pollinated (60 days)—The 1939 classic that is still considered the standard variety. Small, light-green pods that are not as woody as other varieties.

'Burgundy' open-pollinated (65 days)—The standard red-podded variety. Pick pods when they are less than 3 inches, or they will be too fibrous.

'Bowling Red'—Large plants that can reach 6 to 8 feet tall in warmer areas, but are much shorter in northern gardens. Dark-red pods are quick to turn tough if not picked when very short—2 to 3 inches long. Makes a good ornamental.

'Alabama Red' open-pollinated (60 days)—Heirloom with fat, light-green pods with a red blush. A favorite in my household.

'Emerald' open-pollinated (55 days)—An old favorite of many, especially in colder climates where it can still grow tall (6 feet). Said to have been popularized by the Campbell's Soup Company in 1950, this okra has long, skinny green pods that can be picked at a larger size without getting woody, and it branches nicely.

'Jambalaya' F1 hybrid (50 days)—The ideal short-season okra for northern growers. It's an early, high producer, and it brings to the kitchen an almost endless supply of green pods. They are best when picked small for pickling, but can be grown up to 4 inches long without becoming woody.

'Perkin's Long Pod' open-pollinated (60 days)—Bright-green, long pods good for gumbo and canning.

'Hill Country Heirloom Red'—An okra with very thick and short pods that have a reddish blush. Pretty in the garden.

OPPOSITE: From left to right, starting in the top left: 'Hill Country Heirloom Red', 'Burmese' heirloom, 'Clemson Spineless', 'Burgundy Red', 'Alabama Red', 'Jing Orange', 'Mayan' heirloom okra (bottom center). Bottom left and right: In the north, okra perform well with a warm kickstart when grown in large pots. They produce attractive plants as well.

TOMATOES, POTATOES, PEPPERS, AND OTHER NIGHTSHADES

The delicious (and sometimes deadly) crops within the family Solanaceae have struggled to overcome a problematic history caused by more than a few black sheep within the family. The nightshades, as they are commonly known, include deadly belladonna, tobacco, and many other species containing alkaloids, which are believed to negatively affect the health of some people. However, most folks trust the clan, and crave the addictive deliciousness offered by the family, which is quite possibly the most popular of all summer vegetable crops. Imagine summer without colorful, warm-from-the-garden heirloom tomatoes, spicy salsa with hot chili peppers, or a winter roast without creamy mashed potatoes. Remember— *belladonna* does translate to "beautiful woman" in Italian.

TOMATOES
Solanum lycopersicum

There may be no other vegetable (or fruit, technically) that has redefined what and how we cook and eat more than the tomato. It took 50 years to move the tomato from the back of the garage to the front lawn, but the tomato has evolved from being a ho-hum crop that your retired grandfather fussed over to a very hip collectible, with a fandom that rivals that of artisanal hops or even chili peppers. These days, seeds of "new" heirlooms are shared or sold in secret online chatrooms and on countless seed-saver lists. The tomato today appeals to all, from bearded dudes who host tasting parties to garden bloggers who share every detail about their 'Green Zebras', 'Mortgage Lifters', and 'Blue Bumblebees'. Finally, pot has met its match, and it's completely legal.

ORIGIN

It's surprising how late the tomato came into the realm of global cuisine—imagine Italian food without the tomato. Or Spanish food. Or just about any cuisine, really. But like beans and potatoes, the tomato is a New World plant, one that didn't reach Europe until after Columbus. It's remarkable, really, how the tomato spread so quickly—especially because it was believed for many years to be toxic. In fact, the genus to which tomatoes belong, Solanum, contains

many plants that are highly toxic, so the fear of poisoning was not without merit. Kudos to the first brave soul who decided to test the theory. Related to other nightshades like potato, pepper, eggplant, and even tobacco, the tomato is native to the South American Pacific coastal nations. Its wild form is believed to have first been used by the Maya and the Aztecs. Most agree that the tomato was not domesticated until much later, however, and bore little similarity to the familiar fruit we know today. The genetic ancestors of *Solanum lycopersicum* still exist in small populations in the Atacama Desert, high in the Andes in northern Chile. Because plant breeders and botanists are eager to reintroduce some of the vigor and genetic traits of these wild plants lost to our modern varieties, seed from these throwback plants is eagerly collected and analyzed. This effort is a main reason why the newest hybrids are far better in the garden when it comes to disease resistance than older domesticated varieties, such as heirlooms, which often succumb to disease long before newer varieties do. But then again, they more than make up for this with their flavors and colors.

The modern tomato (heirlooms included here) lacks many of the genetic traits of the true wild tomato species, most notably those that aid in fighting disease and viruses. If your tomato crops are plagued by late blight or Verticillium wilt, we can only blame ourselves for overbreeding these plants. The solution is to opt for the

OPPOSITE: 'Red Zebra'

newest disease-resistant cultivars that have a VF in front of their name, signifying their resistance to both Verticillium wilt and Fusarium wilt. When it comes to avoiding the dreaded late blight, however, little can be done except to rotate crops and pray for a dry summer.

Supermarket tomatoes today offer just a shadow of what a garden-grown tomato brings to the plate, but nevertheless they are much better than they were a generation ago. Advances in plant science and breeding, along with innovative growing methods, have improved the supermarket tomato to a point that's quite close to a summer-flavored garden tomato. Close, but not the same.

Entire books have been written on the single topic of raising tomatoes. There is no shortage of advice—tomato-growing "secrets" range from grinding up eggshells and Epsom salts to peeing on your plants, but horticulturally, the tomato's basic needs are simple to understand.

Tomatoes are not tricky, but mastering them can take you down a rabbit hole where advice is often contradictory. Novelty methods abound, from growing plants on hay bales to hanging them in upside-down planters. Many of these techniques work to a point, as the tomato is botanically a vine, and thus resilient and vigorous in a multitude of garden conditions, if offered some basic sunlight and water. But to truly master growing tomatoes, a little homework will be rewarded when it comes to the plant's exact needs.

CHOOSING VARIETIES

Growing great tomatoes begins with choosing the varieties you want. There are endless sources for tomatoes online and in catalogs, with thousands of varieties available, from the tiniest currant types (*S. pimpinellifolium*) to giant beefsteaks (*S. lycopersicum*). Heirloom varieties are often preferred for flavor, as well as for their incredible colors and shapes, while new hybrids offer uniformity, thinner skins, and traits like less splitting and better storage.

Given this range, experts divide tomatoes into broad groups based on size, which is also how most seed catalogs organize them. They also are grouped as being either determinate or indeterminate. This reflects how

they grow. Determinate types are bush types, requiring little staking. This usually refers to early blooming, early harvest varieties. Indeterminates are essentially climbing tomatoes. More vinelike, they require more pruning to reduce their rampant growth. This group includes most tomatoes, and usually all the heirloom types.

While heirloom tomatoes offer the most diversity, do not dismiss modern hybrids. Include them as part of your tomato-planting scheme, especially if you have had issues with late blight and other diseases. Any GMO fears should be dismissed, as there are no GMO tomatoes. Hybrid varieties offer many benefits, such as disease resistance and general vigor that heirlooms can lack. Most experienced gardeners choose to grow both heirlooms and new hybrids.

Tomato varieties include cherry and grape types, paste (or plum/Roma) types, beefsteaks, and the standard globe shapes. More quirky types include the old-fashioned ox-hearts or stuffing tomatoes, which should not be overlooked due to their hollow shells. Seed companies are aware of current trends, and thus are offering more and more of these "artisan tomatoes." These colorful heirlooms include many other types, including odd-looking ribbed or lobed tomatoes, fuzzy peach tomatoes, super-sweet currant type (known as 'Pimp's'), and long sausage-shaped tomatoes. A small garden can provide the kitchen with a rainbow of colors, ranging from dark-red and pink tomatoes to ones that are almost pure white, or even black. Some tomatoes are striped, speckled, or completely green when ripe. There are also dwarf or "patio" types, which offer a smaller-sized plant for those with limited space.

STARTING FROM SEED

Starting your own plants from seed is my recommended way to grow tomatoes (and most other plants). Plan early by ordering seed trays and containers in late winter, when you order your seeds. Make sure to have plenty of good, professional-grade potting soil. It's a fair investment, but a bale of sterile, well-balanced soil is the foundation of robust, healthy plants. Don't forget the little things, like plastic labels and a paintpen or pencil that won't fade.

Sowing seed too early and growing too many plants are the most common mistakes seed-starters make. A good strategy is to grow three or four seeds of each variety you will plant. This allows you to raise many different varieties, even in a small garden, rather than just two or three types. Embrace the diversity.

The best place to germinate your seedlings may be a different spot than the best place to raise them. Choose a warm place indoors where you can set a tray of tomatoes to germinate. Tomatoes demand high temperatures to germinate well—between 70°F and 90°F. This can be accomplished with an electric propagation mat, or you can improvise by setting a seed tray on top of a refrigerator. I set mine above the range in the kitchen on a stainless-steel restaurant shelf. Trays only need to remain in this warm spot until they germinate, which is normally between 6 and 10 days.

Sow tomatoes indoors 6 to 8 weeks before you plan on setting them out. Factor in a week or so as a hardening-off period, when trays of individual seedlings can be set out to acclimate to outdoor conditions. A local university with an agricultural department may be able to offer specific dates for your area, but a reasonable calculation is to count back from your region's frost-free date, and then add 2 weeks.

STARTING CONTAINERS

While seeds will grow in almost anything that will hold soil, rather than taking the novelty route of using eggshells or egg cartons, try to use new plastic containers

So many heirloom tomato varieties come into our kitchen in late August that our friends look forward to our annual tomato tasting party, where we taste-test and vote on our favorites (usually a tie between 'Sudduth's Brandywine' and one of the many 'Mortgage Lifter' varieties.

MASTERING TECHNIQUES
TIPS FOR GROWING TOMATOES

- Tomatoes that are set out into the garden in late spring, when it has fully warmed, tend to fare better.
- Homegrown seedlings or smaller transplants often produce larger and healthier plants.
- Growing disease-resistant varieties can reduce the chances of late blight.
- Container-grown crops are a good option in home gardens if crop rotation is impractical.
- Tomatoes from garden centers often are treated with growth regulators to appear healthier, with thicker stems and stocky growth, which may affect early performance at home.
- Tomatoes succumb to late blight for many reasons, as the spores are airborne. Outbreaks can often be delayed with sanitary precautions.
- Tomatoes split due to irregular watering (dry periods followed by soaking).
- Blossom-end rot is usually brought on by stress and low calcium uptake due to improper soil pH.
- Plants that grow lush and green but produce little fruit probably suffer from over-fertility (too much nitrogen) or reduced sunlight.
- Tomato yields are lower if you do not prune vines to reduce their growth.
- Rotating tomato crops and not reusing old soil in containers may be the best way to avoid diseases with tomato plants. If you have a small garden, alternating from containers to raised beds and back again every other year helps keep down late blight.

that can be washed out and sterilized with bleach and water (1 teaspoon per gallon). Yogurt containers with drainage holes will certainly work, but some studies indicate that roots may grow best in a dark (i.e. black plastic) container, so it may be wise to invest in plastic cell trays or, better yet, individual pots that fit into a tray, available online at wholesale grower sites. Uniformity makes managing lots of pots easier.

Professional growers and ambitious amateurs use plug trays for starting tomatoes. The tiny tray cells are filled with an expert starting mix, watered well, and house one seed each, set in a ⅛-inch-deep hole using tweezers. Once the first set of leaves unfolds, each seedling can be removed by poking through the drainage hole below with a pencil or chopstick, and with very little root disturbance at all, it can be set into its final growing pot—a 4-inch black pot. This will be an easier task if you allow the cell to dry first—that's exactly how the professional growers do it.

Don't forget labels. While wood ones look very nice, white plastic tends to withstand the elements better and stay readable, as long as you use a waterproof permanent marker, paint pen or pencil. When you plant multiple varieties (which I strongly recommend), it is very frustrating when your tomato plant labels disappear or are destroyed. You might assume you can tell them apart, but even after the fruit is mature, it can be surprisingly difficult to tell which is which. If you forgot to order labels, write on the pot with a white paint pen.

GROWING SEEDLINGS INDOORS
When your first tomato seedlings emerge, move the tray under a grow light, which can be set relatively close to the plants for maximum light and heat. In a greenhouse, this isn't a worry—natural sunlight is preferred. But in the

OPPOSITE: Colorful, high-season heirloom tomatoes will seem to come in all at once. Sharing with friends and neighbors if they become over-abundant is always welcome. Few will care if they are less-perfect irregular shapes, and though stress damage often comes without warning, it rarely affects flavor.

average home, even a south-facing window may not be as bright as a lighting unit.

It's essential to use a light timer, as tomato seedlings are day-length sensitive. Set the timer for 16 hours of light to get the best results. A temperature differential, if slight, is beneficial as long as it is not too extreme—shifts of more than 10°F can cause seedlings to grow lanky. Greenhouses try to maintain only a slight difference between day and night temperatures with tomato crops.

A good nutrition program is important for almost any plant, but particularly for tomatoes. While seedlings are indoors and still young, I use a balanced 8-8-8 water-soluble, chemical-based fertilizer. It's quick to absorb and fast-acting. Organic feeds are better for outdoors in the garden where there are organisms present to help make the feed accessible to plants (most are slow-acting). Fish emulsion is problematic due to its high nitrogen levels and tendency to attract fungus gnats. If you do get fungus gnats (they look like fruit flies and live in the top slime layer of the soil often in seed trays), allow the surface of the soil to dry out between waterings, and reduce the amount of organic fertilizer. Worst-case scenarios require transplanting into clean soil—never use cinnamon or any of the folk remedies often suggested.

Transplant seedlings into 4-inch pots just as they are forming their first true set of leaves (a time when young seedlings can tolerate transplanting much better than older ones). Young seedling tomatoes are quite tolerant of root disturbance, so transplanting even from a tangled mess of seedlings often doesn't hurt the plants. Once three sets of leaves form, however, things get complicated, and plants tend to suffer more from transplanting.

BUYING TOMATO STARTS

While I am a very strong advocate for home-growing your tomato plants from seed, it is undeniable that most home gardeners don't take the time to grow seedlings inside their house or greenhouse. Tomato plants are available at almost every garden center, and it won't take you long to become familiar with the many varieties that are available.

- Look for tomato plants with two or three pairs of leaves, as this is the ideal size for transplanting.
- Avoid plants with flowers and those with small fruits, no matter how tempting they may seem. Unless it is August, these fruits won't develop properly.
- A plant that has been grown stress-free will have vibrant, dark-green foliage, while those that have been exposed to damaging stressors may have yellowish leaves.
- A well-grown transplant will have roots that are just reaching the sides of the container, and it should come out easily (if not, allow the container to dry a bit).

PLANTING, STAKING, AND PRUNING

Botanically, the tomato is a vine. This helps us understand why it is remarkably resilient and vigorous but, at the same time, must be pruned wisely and staked soundly. But first you need to get it from the pot into the ground. And that starts with prepping the soil.

Growing soil. Starting with pH, most of us don't need to worry about well-balanced garden soil, but know that an acidic soil with a pH below 5.5 will encourage more diseases, such as the dreaded Fusarium wilt and pathogen molds like Botrytis. An overly high pH (above 8.0) will also encourage diseases of types like Verticillium wilt. As there is no across-the-board advice for every gardener, the safest thing to do is to get a professional soil test done and see where your soil sits.

Planting. Indeterminate tomatoes should be spaced a full 3 feet apart. Dig the planting hole slightly deeper than the root ball, but not so deep that the lower branches of the plant are covered. Lightly pack soil around the rootball and crown. Ground horticultural

TOP LEFT: 'Reisetomate'. **TOP CENTER:** 'Dark Galaxy'. **TOP RIGHT**: 'Green Zebra'. **MIDDLE LEFT:** 'Atomic Grape'.
MIDDLE CENTER: 'Red Currant'. **MIDDLE RIGHT:** 'Berkeley Tie-Dye Green'.

limestone can be added to each hole before planting if your soil test indicates an acid soil (below 5.0). Tomatoes prefer a pH range between 6.0 and 7.5. Within this range, the plant can take up necessary nutrients as it makes minerals that help control blossom-end rot. Water immediately.

Staking. There are many ways to stake a tomato plant, from simple wooden stakes and twine to elaborate cages and teepees. Whole volumes have been written on this topic, and every gardener has his or her favorite method. Whatever method you choose, be sure to support the branches so they don't snap under the weight of the heavy fruit, keep the fruit off the ground, and allow air to circulate through the plant (poor air circulation can lead to many ailments).

Fertilizing. Tomato plants respond well to light feeding and fertile soil, but you can easily overfeed plants. When this happens, they may look healthy, but you can forget about a heavy fruit set. Ideally, use a half-strength feed lower in nitrogen once plants are in the soil. If using a soilless mix to reduce pathogens in containers, more frequent feeding may be required than with plants grown in regular, fertile garden soil. Tomatoes are rather forgiving when it comes to fertility, but there are some ground rules. I say that it's best to feed plants if they appear pale or weak, which happens more often in containers than in the garden. Often the case with container plants is that the soil has become too acidic, especially if you try to reuse old soil from a previous year. Amending old soil with ground lime may be necessary, or better yet, replace it with soil from a fresh bag.

Pruning. The benefits of pruning are simple to understand—your plants will produce better-quality fruit of the right size if the vines are pruned to reduce rampant growth. No benefit comes from keeping the plant unpruned, as axillary stems forming at every leaf node will quickly take over, leaving you with a very healthy-looking foliage plant, but one with practically no blossoms

or fruit. These axillary stems can easily be snapped off in the early morning, or cut with scissors (tomato geeks will even wipe the scissors with alcohol after every cut to avoid transferring disease). Check plants every few days in midsummer as new stems will form practically overnight. When the stems have reached the top of your staking material, snap off the growing tip. An indeterminate variety (that's most of them) will grow on and on without stopping, so you need to manually stop them at some point to allow the plant to focus on maturing fruit.

TOMATO POLLINATION

Contrary to popular belief, tomatoes are self-pollinating. Bees are not necessary to perform the pollination task, as each flower contains both the male and female parts. That's not to say that bees and other pollinators don't help, but poor fruit set usually has more to do with temperature and humidity than with the flowers failing to do their duty. As desert plants in the wild, tomatoes are more sensitive to humidity than you may think. Too much humidity combined with hot temperatures (above 95°F) can make the pollen grains sticky—they simply drop to the ground, too heavy to become windborne.

Tomatoes that live their entire life in a greenhouse may need bees to aid with pollination, or perhaps a careful tickle with a paintbrush. But in the garden, the wind and the blossom structure usually do the job.

AVOIDING TOMATO STRESSORS

Tomatoes are highly sensitive to stressors such as poor nutrition, improper soil pH, drought, temperature swings, and extreme temperatures (above 95°F or below 55°F), any of which can cause weak fruit set. Setting plants out later in the early summer, once the soil has warmed and nighttime temperatures remain above 65°F, will help avoid many of these stressors. Tomatoes are also prone to dropping their flowers when daytime temperatures get too hot—above 90°F—or when nighttime temperatures dip below 55°F. These extremes will render the pollen sterile, and this is a good reason never to buy a plant with blossoms or fruit too early in the spring.

It's a good idea to grow a mix of colorful heirlooms as well as some disease-resistant hybrids to ensure an abundant harvest come late summer. Ending up with a rainbow of varieties to serve is one of the most rewarding aspects of raising many varieties of tomatoes.

POTATOES

The indigenous Andean tuber we know today as the ubiquitous potato is perhaps the most common of the solanum—or nightshade—tribe. While few think about the history of this vegetable beyond its relationship to the tragic Irish Potato Famine in the mid-nineteenth century, the crop's value stretches back in time much further than most realize. The potato has a history of 10,000 years in the high Andes of Bolivia and Peru, where it is still an important staple. Early European explorers, including Sir Francis Drake, first brought the potato to the rest of the world.

While ancient landrace potato varieties still exist in some Andean mountain valleys, the potato has been transformed by careful selection and modern breeding into a much blander but more useful (and safer) crop to eat.

WHY GROW POTATOES?

Quality is the main reason to consider growing potatoes. Because they are inexpensive vegetables, you won't save much money growing potatoes at home, but do it for the flavor and texture. Any variety you choose to grow has tremendous value in the kitchen. Serve a plate of mashed, fresh-from-the-garden tubers, and your eyes will roll back in delight.

OPPOSITE: Growing your own potatoes is highly rewarding as potatoes fresh from the ground are incredibly delicious and a treat few ever get to experience.

Fresh potatoes are rarely experienced by most people. Dug in the late summer or autumn, they are crisp, firm, and waxy just out of the soil, and like wine, offer a unique terroir specific to your garden.

SOURCING SEED POTATOES

The term "seed potato" is confusing, as they are not truly seed—only potato breeders raise potatoes from real seed. "Seed potato" refers to a potato grown specifically for planting in the garden. These are available in the early spring from many sources—from farm supply stores to some mail-order seed catalogs.

Although in theory you can plant supermarket potatoes that have begun to sprout in the spring, it is not recommended. Growth can be very irregular, as commercially grown potatoes are treated with a growth retardant that prevents them from performing well. Because raising potatoes is a 6-month effort and still cheap even if you splurge on seed potatoes, why not go for the highest quality plant material to maximize your results?

Seed potatoes ordered online from reputable seed suppliers are often the freshest, as they are shipped to your home at the proper time for planting in late winter or early spring. Potatoes dislike hot weather and may even fail when temperatures remain above 90°F for an extended period (remember, they come from the high An-

While the potato saved whole populations from famine because of its high productivity and ease of growth, it was these very qualities that helped cause one of the most impactful famines of all: the Irish Potato Famine. Over-reliance on a monoculture made most of nineteenth-century Europe vulnerable, but the direct cause of the Irish calamity stemmed from guano shipments that introduced *Phytophthora infestans*—a water mold or oomycete that quickly multiplied in the summer of 1845, wiping out crops of potatoes across Europe.

Despite the lessons learned from the Potato Famine, issues with monoculture continue to plague us today. But the event also led to innovations in the then-emerging science of insecticides, with the creation of new treatments that were more effective, but not necessarily safe. One such insecticide was Paris green, a toxic blend of arsenic and copper that was developed after the famine and recommended to treat potato, tomato, and other crops vulnerable to the now worldwide *Phytophthora infestans*. Today, we continue to fight this disease that plagues many home vegetable crops in the nightshade family— particularly potatoes and tomatoes. Little can be done once the spores are released in your garden during hot and humid spells in midsummer, but you can sometimes control the damage by choosing resistant varieties of plants or by treating the foliage with a copper-based spray.

des mountains, like tomatoes). Therefore, raising crops in the winter from an autumn sowing is advisable for those in warmer climates.

PREPARATION

Upon delivery, the tubers should be sorted and cut into 1½ to 2-inch pieces with a sharp knife, making sure that each piece has an "eye" or small bud on it. Take great care not to scratch off any of these buds if they are beginning to swell. Many growers allow their seed potatoes to sit in a brightly lit area to allow the small potatoes to first sprout a bit. This is called "chitting" or "to chit the potatoes." This is helpful for northern gardeners who may find that waiting for the garden soil to reach 50°F takes longer than planned.

Soil preparation is essential, although potatoes are not fussy and can grow in most any medium—even straw if kept irrigated. But if you are serious about raising potatoes, it's worth the effort to prepare the soil properly—it will maximize your harvest.

The most common error I've seen is the addition of ground limestone to the soil in spring. I've even seen agricultural supply stores selling bags of dolomitic limestone next to crates of potato seed, which can be confusing. Potatoes are one of the few crops that prefer acidic soil, ideally with a soil pH of 4.8 to 5.5.

While potatoes will grow and yield in even average soil, with a little tweaking, crops can be remarkably productive. Potatoes are heavy feeders, and many gardeners go wrong by following novel methods or simply not fertilizing at all, perhaps believing they are raising a healthier spud without fertilizer. The results will be disappointing, with small, deformed tubers and a low yield. If you want high-quality food, raise high-quality plants and provide them with the conditions they need to grow optimally.

As with many vegetables in the home garden, understanding nutrient needs and introducing a management program can greatly improve your harvest. Start by breaking down the main growth stages of the potato into three phases:

the vegetative stage (when the plants are just forming leaves), the tuber-forming stage (when little potatoes are just starting to form), and the tuber-bulking stage (when the potatoes are swelling up and maturing). During each of these stages, the potato plant has different nutritional needs.

What makes feeding potatoes a bit more complex is your soil pH. While potato growers know that the crop thrives in acidic soil (which also helps reduce outbreaks of common potato scab disease), acidic soil renders many essential nutrients inactive. Thus, potato plants can experience some nutrient deficiencies unless you adjust the soil in other ways—mainly with fertilizer. If you've ever been disappointed with your potato crop, then a few tweaks in what you feed them may help.

Going back to the three phases of the potato's life cycle helps us understand what's going on under the soil. Most blends of fertilizer depend on nitrogen to carry most of the weight, and while nitrogen is also crucial for potatoes, it is less important than the other elements. In fact, too much nitrogen can weaken a plant and cause it to focus more on creating leaves rather than tubers. Potatoes mainly need nitrogen in their first phase of growing, until they form flowers. If in doubt, check the NPK analysis and make sure that the first number of the three is lower than the others.

With potatoes, it's all about the second stage of tuber-forming. This happens just as the potatoes begin to flower. It is then that the plants need less nitrogen but plenty of phosphorus and potassium—two nutrients many forget to think about, especially when feeding with fish emulsion or a water-soluble chemical feed. Each of these has their place in the garden, but not at this phase with potatoes.

Phosphorus is found at garden centers and nurseries, where it is usually sold as phosphate or superphosphate. Organic forms of phosphate include bone meal or rock phosphate, and while they may seem like a smarter choice, they require some forethought—these are slow-release in nature, and potatoes are fast-growing and need quick access to these nutrients if they are to metabolize them. Manure is very helpful in creating the ideal soil for potatoes, but it too must be applied in the late fall or winter. I dump duck and chicken manure on my potato beds all

winter and dig it in as soon as the snow melts, augmenting with potassium sulfate and wood ash. If you have a friend with horses or chickens, exploit the friendship to include manure in trade for potatoes. Adding straw and manure through a snowy winter will render the soil ideal.

If opting to buy chemical-based fertilizer, look for granular forms of ammonium sulfate (often sold in bags as superphosphate or even smaller amounts of triple superphosphate) and apply it in early spring according to the packaging directions. Conventional potato farmers and competitive growers will dig a 0-0-50 into the ground just when they are planting seed potatoes. For the home grower, a ratio of one handful per plant seems to do the trick in most cases, but competitive growers in the United Kingdom often add a few handfuls of phosphorous to the bottom of each planting container. Note that nitrogen is more likely than phosphorus to burn a plant.

MAINTAINING THE CROP

Potatoes at this point may seem like a lot of work, but even though there are some essential early steps, for much of the season you can leave the crop alone. Once plants are hilled, all that's left is cultivating the rows, weeding, and watering.

Hilling confuses many new gardeners, but it is a simple task. Hilling refers to pulling up the soil a few inches with a hoe around each plant. This is done after the potato plants emerge from the soil, and it's important because the roots that form from the stem into the hilled soil are where potato tubers form, and these tubers cannot be exposed to sunlight. If sown in a 6-inch trench, pulling a bit of soil around each plant 4 weeks after they have emerged is an easy task. You only have to hill the plants once or twice at the beginning of the growth cycle, and probably not at all once they bloom. It's worth noting that some additional hilling can be beneficial if any tubers become exposed after hard summer rains.

Weeding is essential. While few weeds will reach the height of a potato plant, their roots are often shallow and will compete with tuber formation. Some care should be taken while weeding, and many growers opt to hand-weed rather than use a cultivation tool, in order to avoid damaging tubers that form close to the surface.

PESTS AND DISEASE

While avoiding the dreaded late blight has already been explained under tomatoes, the use of a fungicide like Actinovate (organic) or copper may delay an outbreak of this disease. Insect damage is limited to the Colorado potato beetle. Only in the smallest gardens does it make sense to handpick or squish the egg cases found under the leaves. The best method to avoid this pest is to use a floating row cover set over wire hoops in early summer paired with crop rotation.

HARVESTING

Summer crops of potatoes should be dug in the late summer or the fall, once the plants above ground have died. Special pitchforks with flattened tines have been designed to prevent piercing the underground potatoes. Or you can just dig carefully, starting a foot or so away from the stem of the plant and using a gentle touch, turning over the soil to reveal the treasures below.

The process of digging without harming the tubers can be a pleasurable task, and many gardeners list this

VARIETIES

FINGERLING TYPE

'Russian Banana' (80 days)—A larger fingerling with good performance and high yields. Pale-yellow flesh and skin.

'French Fingerling' (75 days)—A lovely pink-skinned fingerling type with pale-yellow flesh and a nice waxy interior.

STORAGE TYPE

'Elba' (80 days)—A large buff-colored waxy potato with pure-white flesh. Resistant to scab.

'Norkotah' (85 days)—A russet potato that performs well in small home gardens.

'Dark Red Norland' (80 days)—Classic red-skinned potato that is reliable and high-yielding in home gardens. Resistant to many viruses and scab.

'Mountain Rose' (78 days)—A beautiful potato with rose-colored flesh and skin. Not as productive as 'Red Norland', but makes up for it with its beauty.

'Purple Majesty' (125 days)—A dark-purple Peruvian-type potato with lovely, exceptionally dark flesh that is high in antioxidants.

'Masquerade' (110 days)—A multicolored potato with mottled pale-yellow and purple skin over waxy, pale-yellow flesh.

as one of their favorite jobs in the garden—it seems like magic when such tangible products of your efforts emerge from the soil.

Dry freshly dug potatoes on trays for a few hours, but for no longer than a day. If you rinsed off any soil with water, be sure that the potatoes are completely dry before storing them in complete darkness. Most gardeners will eat their homegrown potatoes within a month, but larger gardens may deliver enough to store in the cellar or a dark crate in a cool closet. Daylight is the potato tuber's greatest enemy.

FROM TOP TO BOTTOM: 'Yukon Gold', 'Dark Red Norland', 'Adirondack Blue', 'Russian Banana', and 'French Fingerling'.

PEPPERS

Capsicum pubescens, C. frutescens,
C. chinense, C. annuum, C. baccatum

Next to tomatoes, the pepper clan has perhaps the most active global fan base. It's no wonder, because peppers are immensely colorful and exciting on many levels—some may even say that they are sensual (well, they certainly can affect one's senses!). Few vegetables have captured the imagination of humankind as much as the pepper. An essential ingredient in regional dishes that fan outward from the equator, the pepper delivers its punch to cuisines of many areas, including Mexico, Central and South America, India, China, and Southeast Asia. Historically, the pepper is not as old as you may think. We can thank the Spanish conquistadors for introducing the pepper to the rest of the world after "discovering" its use in indigenous diets throughout South America.

With flavor profiles ranging from sweet and fruity to smoky and chocolatey to pungent and searing-hot, the pepper is one of the most popular and studied plants you can grow in the home garden.

ORGANIZING PEPPERS

All peppers are organized by botanists under the genus *Capsicum*, in which there are nearly 30 species. Most domesticated peppers fall into five distinct species, and knowing the species will help you understand a pepper's cultural needs, as not all peppers require the same culture. For example, many of the *C. frutescens* and *C. annuum* var. *glabriusculum* (the Pequin and Tepin types) can survive for years indoors, either allowed to enter a state of semi-dormancy in a cool cellar or kept on a cool windowsill.

THE FIVE DOMESTICATED PEPPER SPECIES ARE:

- *Capsicum pubescens*—This includes the rocoto peppers found in the high Andes mountains. These are a bit more cold-hardy and are popular with pepper enthusiasts, who overwinter them indoors in pots so the plants can continue to grow.
- *Capsicum frutescens*—The tabasco types including the tiny 'African Bird's Eye', 'Malagueta', and 'Siling Labuyo'.
- *Capsicum chinense*—These have become very popular with hot-sauce enthusiasts. The species includes all of the lantern-shaped, warm-weather-growing, long-season types such as habanero, Scotch bonnets, and Bhut

OPPOSITE: Green bell peppers are common, but just because they are familiar doesn't mean there are better peppers to try in the home garden. There are plenty you will never find in markets. Try 'Islander', a tender purple bell pepper, or 'Bianca', an ivory-colored one. Both are mild and sweet with tender skins crisp from the garden. 'Biscayne' is a wonderful Cubanelle-type great for frying but also for eating fresh in salads.

MASTERING TECHNIQUES
TIPS FOR GROWING PEPPERS

- Compacted soil encourages weak growth, so take steps to keep soil soft and loose.
- A raised bed with plastic mulch is a great environment for peppers.
- Add calcium (applied as a liquid feed) to combat blossom-end rot.
- Bell peppers, like tomatoes, won't set fruit if the weather is too hot (above 90°F) or too cold (below 60°F), so timing is key in getting young plants into the garden in early summer.

jolokia, as well as the scorpion types, the famed ghost peppers, and the 'Carolina Reapers'.

- *Capsicum annuum*—This species is broken down into two varieties: *C. annuum* var. *glabriusculum*, which covers the tiny, dark, North American 'Pequin' and chiltepin types, and *C. annuum* var. *annuum,* which are the most common peppers in the bell pepper tribe—'Fresno' types, Hungarian wax, poblano, serrano, and shishito.

- *Capsicum baccatum*—These originated in ancient Peru and include the oddly shaped yet beautiful 'Bishop's Crown' types, 'Starfish' types, 'Peppadew', 'Lemon Drop', and 'Sugar Rush'. These are often referred to as aji peppers in some cultures, as in 'Aji Limon'.

HOT PEPPERS

An entire subculture has emerged around high-capsaicin chili peppers as more and more fans try to outdo each other in eating the hottest pepper in the world or in making the hottest hot sauce. Once little-known varieties like ghost peppers and 'Carolina Reapers' have become mainstream and are being embraced for the addictive, if not masochistic, experience of extreme chili pepper collecting. Most home gardeners prefer to dabble with these excruciatingly hot varieties more for their looks than for eating, since most chili pepper plants are as beautiful as any ornamental. With a seemingly endless list of varieties to choose from, the ornamental value of hot peppers is as powerful as their searing punch.

SWEET BELL PEPPERS

While the chili pepper has its fans, the mild bell pepper (along with other *Capsicum annuum* var. *annuum* types) remains the workhorse of the pepper world. Mild green bell peppers and their colorful kin are certainly worth growing in the home garden—like many summer vegetables, the flavor and quality of home-raised peppers are far superior when compared to store-bought peppers.

Bell peppers come in any number of shapes and colors, and each has similar needs in the garden. Many peppers, even bell peppers, do very well when cultivated in containers. Along with their close relatives—the horn-shaped 'Fresno', serrano, and shishito—these peppers are often overlooked as valuable citizens in the garden, if only because garden centers carry a limited list of varieties. Seed catalogs will list dozens of varieties, some new and far better than what you are likely to find at a garden center.

RAISING PEPPERS FROM SEED

Pepper seeds require specialized treatment and take a couple of months to reach transplantable size when raised indoors, but they are not difficult, and with a little attention, you can have a few dozen pepper plants ready to set out into the garden by late spring.

Peppers require heat to germinate well, with a constant soil temperature between 80°F to 90°F. This will require a heating mat, which is a worthy investment for any serious gardener. Even with my heated greenhouse, I must start my pepper seeds indoors. Pepper seedlings tolerate

transplanting well, so you can sow a half-dozen seeds in a 3- or 4-inch container set into a flat with other containers of various pepper types. When pepper seedlings have formed their first pair of leaves, they can be carefully divided and set into individual pots with a sterile soilless mix.

A transplanted seedling will grow sturdier at warmer temperatures of 70°F to 74°F during the day, with a slightly cooler shift at night, dropping down to 68°F. A cold windowsill, even if sunny and bright, may not be the best choice while plants are young if the temperatures dip too low at night. If you are raising pepper plants indoors under fluorescent grow lights, the slight shift to nighttime temperatures when the lights go off may be all they need.

All peppers are strong feeders and like a complete nutrient solution, which is best applied as a liquid feed, especially while the seedlings are young. Fertilize with a 5-5-5 biweekly, or perhaps with a 5-5-10. Pepper seedlings should be encouraged to grow vigorously until they are ready to be set out into the garden. Plant peppers outdoors after all threat of frost has passed, ideally when the soil temperature has reached 60°F.

Don't skimp on fertilizer with pepper plants. Recent research has indicated that peppers grow best not only with a balanced feed (10-10-10), but with additional phosphorus and calcium. Soil should be well-drained and fertile, with additional organic material added before planting out.

'Lunchbox', a rainbow-colored pepper mix.

TRANSPLANTING INTO THE GARDEN

Because pepper seedlings should be grown warm, they must be hardened off before planting into the ground. Setting the pots out on a deck, or even in the garden, for a week or so will strengthen the plants, but be sure to bring them indoors at night if the weather turns. If young pepper plants are just beginning to form buds, then you've reached the optimum time to set plants out into the garden. Peppers have a limited temperature range in which the blossoms are pollinated optimally. They abort at high temperatures.

Getting plants into the ground in late spring or early summer allows them to maximize the ideal temperature range between 65°F and 90°F. Anything higher, and fruit set can be low. If buying plants at a nursery, avoid plants that are too large or are already showing fruit. The perfect pepper transplant is one that is not yet blooming but just beginning to form buds.

The use of black plastic mulch is very helpful in maintaining soil warmth and moisture. Commercial growers water transplants in with a solution high in phosphorus to help roots and plants grow quickly.

PESTS AND DISEASE

If cutworms are a problem in your garden, use cardboard collars or paper collars (made from folded magazine pages) to discourage them. Moisture should be constant, but as peppers enjoy well-drained soil, the use of a drip irrigation system might be helpful, especially if you are using plastic mulch. If not, be sure that a sprinkler can reach open soil around the stem to maintain adequate moisture needs.

Aphids can be problematic on plants raised indoors, but rarely affect plants out in the garden. Treat with mild insecticidal soap or pyrethrum. I am not above hand-squishing some as well.

Late blight can affect peppers, as can bacterial spot and blossom-end rot. Some commercial growers use a product called RootShield®, which is a beneficial fungus that can be introduced into the sterile soil mix or drenched in at seedling stage. It has proven helpful in organically controlling both Pythium and Fusarium.

STAKING AND PRUNING

Pepper experts agree that some pruning and staking is helpful with certain varieties. Many peppers require a sturdy stake, usually bamboo or wood. Aggressive growers should be pruned to three main stems. Pinch out the growing points if the plants seem to be forming too many flower buds and not setting enough fruit. Chili peppers in containers often need to be trimmed to keep plants performing well, and they also need to be staked for support, as heavy peppers weigh the plants down near late summer.

VARIETIES

There are dozens of varieties for each type of pepper to satisfy every kind of pepper enthusiast. Nurseries may sell peppers just by type, as we find them in markets labeled along the lines of jalapeño, cubanelle, or habanero. But learning about the many named varieties available from seed is fun and educational. Here are a few favorites.

BELL PEPPERS

'Ace' F1—A good, standard bell pepper for green or red peppers in the summer—even for northern gardeners.

HOT CHILI PEPPERS

'Mad Hatter' F1—An AAS winner that improves upon many of the qualities found in any of the hot bishop's hat or starfish-shaped peppers. Only slightly hot (I can eat this one fresh!) and very pretty as a tall container plant.

'El Jefe' F1—An excellent early jalapeño good for cooler gardens or in the north.

'Hot Rod' F1—A serrano type that produces plenty of fruit. Great for summer salsas and useful elsewhere in the kitchen.

'Padron' or 'Shishito'—Rather new on the scene in the West, these are thin-skinned, mild peppers that have become very trendy, served fried in a cast-iron pan and sprinkled with sea salt and olive oil. They say one in a hundred is deadly hot, but I have yet to encounter one.

EGGPLANT

Solanum melongena

Botanists have lumped eggplants (also known as aubergines) together into a botanical group referred to as "the spiny solanums." If you have ever worked with eggplants yourself, you know exactly why—on many varieties, the stem, branches, and even the leaves are covered with sharp thorns meant to ward off predators. For eggplant growers, these are easily managed with a good pair of garden gloves, but what really makes the eggplant interesting is its ancestry: the eggplant is one of the few solanums that originated in the Old World.

Botanically, the eggplant fruit is a berry. It dates back to prehistory—it was common in the ancient cuisines of the Middle East and Asia, and is believed to have been introduced to the Iberian Peninsula by the Arabs in the Middle Ages. Many have a love/hate relationship with eggplants. While the eggplant aficionado needs little encouragement to grow these strikingly beautiful vegetables, for others, adding eggplant to a summer garden might take some convincing. While many enjoy the soft texture eggplants add to favorite dishes from Italy, the Middle East, and India, plenty of others find their texture just plain unappealing.

Most think of the eggplant as the iconic dark-purple variety, nearly black with an ovoid shape. But it all depends on where you live. India and Asia have the most diversity of eggplant types, while Italy, Greece, and the Middle East have introduced some of the most beautiful cultivars—some striped, rose-colored, or bicolored. Culinary eggplant, like tomatoes, has been selected from three distinct species: *Solanum melongena*, *S. macrocarpon*, and *S. aethiopicum*—the scarlet eggplant. *S. melongena* is further divided into three common varieties according to form and color. These include: *S. melongena* var. *esculentum*, the common dark-purple and most white varieties; *S. melongena* var. *depressum*, the dwarf eggplants; and *S. melongena* var. *serpentium*, the snake-shaped eggplants.

Like all solanums, eggplant is primarily a warm-weather crop that relishes heat and humidity. A long season is required to achieve strong and heathy plants in the garden, so getting off to a good start indoors helps. So does choosing the proper variety. Nurseries and garden centers have limited varieties, often carrying only one or two 'Black Beauty' types. The adventurous home chef may want something a bit different, such as an heirloom with incredible meatiness like 'Bianca Sfumata di Rosa'; the only way you can reliably obtain these finer varieties is to buy seed and raise a selection yourself.

OPPOSITE: Eggplant varieties, clockwise from the top: 'Rosa Bianca', 'Gretel F1', 'Kazakhstan', 'Patio Baby', 'Nubia' variegated Italian, 'White Fingers', 'Tsakoniki Greek', 'Orient Charm' F1, 'Hansel', and 'Thai Long Green' in center.

RAISING FROM SEED

The benefits of raising most vegetables from seed are many, but with eggplants, it comes down to control. If you favor organic methods, start your eggplant seedlings at home from organic seed. Eggplant seedlings are often treated with growth regulators as recommended by commercial seed distributors. Consumers should question nursery staff if plants were pretreated or not, especially when buying vegetable starts. Typically, homegrown plants will grow larger, often requiring staking in support of the magnificent specimen's display.

Start seeds early indoors at least 6 to 8 weeks before the last frost date. Sow seeds ¼ inch deep, and cover with a sterile soilless mix. The use of a heated propagation mat is very helpful, as eggplant seeds require continually warm soil temperatures (near 90°F) until they germinate. If setting trays under artificial lights, the addition of a heating mat will help keep the soil warm when the lights are shut off. Once seedlings emerge, the temperatures can drop to between 65°F and 70°F.

Eggplant seedlings can handle transplanting well while young, which allows the home grower to start a few seeds in each pot or sprout rows within a larger seed tray, and then transplant them later into 3- to 4-inch pots. If growing more than one variety, be sure to label each pot or row since seedlings often look very similar. Harden young plants off by bringing outdoors for 1 to 2 weeks on mild days in late spring—this will acclimate them to wind and full sunshine. With such a wide variety of eggplants to choose from, don't be afraid to plant a few seeds of multiple varieties.

EGGPLANTS IN CONTAINERS

Like many solanums, eggplants perform very well in containers and are attractive enough to be used as ornamental plants. Many have beautiful lavender flowers, and they certainly bear interestingly shaped, colorful fruit. Two plants can be set into 14-inch terra cotta pots that you can place along a driveway or a walkway, saving garden space for other crops.

EGGPLANTS IN THE GARDEN

Fertility balance, heat, and spacing are the keys to success with eggplant crops. Soils that are rich in organic matter are ideal, but be careful with later applications of fertilizer. An abundance of nitrogen will stimulate foliar growth rather than fruit set. A liquid feed higher in phosphorus than nitrogen and drenched-in at planting time will be all that is needed in most soils. Try 2-5-3 or any feed in which the second and third numbers are largest on the fertilizer package.

Eggplants have few pests in home gardens, but flea beetles and Colorado potato beetles can be problems in some areas. Flea beetles make small holes in the leaves, and Colorado potato beetles lay eggs on the undersides of the leaves. These can be crushed by hand (or by eager children), and all can be reduced by using a floating row cover. On mature plants these outbreaks are more cosmetic than damaging, affecting only the appearance of the leaves, but not the fruit. Sometimes it's best to tolerate the holes in the leaves rather than spraying.

Staking is often needed, as the fruits are very heavy. Also, eggplant is sensitive to cool periods—commercial growers often use floating row covers to provide extra heat and control insects.

VARIETIES

ASIAN LONG TYPE

'Orient Express' F1 hybrid (58 days)—An early-producing variety good for cool-weather climates, it also produces under heat stress. Skinny, darkest-purple eggplants are 8 to 10 inches long.

'Orient Charm' F1 hybrid (65 days)—A lighter-purple long eggplant suitable for containers or raised beds. Unlike 'Orient Express', which has dark-purple calyxes, 'Orient Charm' has green.

'Calliope' F1 hybrid (64 days)—A short, oval, bicolored eggplant that can be picked very small at 2 inches as baby fruit, or larger at 4 inches. Purple and white stripes.

ITALIAN TYPE

'Barbarella' F1 hybrid (65 days)—Large 4- to 5-inch roundish yet pleated fruit that are dark purple, fading to white near the calyx end.

'Hansel' F1 hybrid (55 days)—This AAS winner grows well in both containers and small gardens, producing 4- to 5-inch fruits that are thin. The 30-inch-tall plants are productive.

'Gretel' F1 hybrid (55 days)—The white counterpart to 'Hansel'. Also an AAS winner with all of the characteristics of 'Hansel', but with snow-white fruit.

'Classic' F1 hybrid (76 days)—The classic large, violet Italian eggplant (an improved variety from 'Black Beauty'). Ideal for eggplant parmesan and for baking.

LEFT: 'Calliope', an Indian-style eggplant. **MIDDLE:** 'Hansel' F1, an AAS winner with abundant crops. **RIGHT:** 'Beatrice' F1, a bright violet Italian-type.

TOMATILLOS AND HUSK CHERRIES

Physalis alkekengi, P. philadelphica, P. ixocarpa

Lesser known in the solanum clan is a tribe of plants grouped as the "husk cherries" or "ground cherries," all within the genus *Physalis*. All species are native to the New World (South and Central America), and it's a surprisingly large genus with nearly 80 species. The age of the genus was revealed in 2017, when a 52-million-year-old fossilized tomatillo was discovered in Patagonia.

The most commonly known ornamental within the group is *Physalis alkekengi*—the Chinese lantern—a bright-orange husk berry once considered a choice (yet somewhat invasive) old-fashioned garden biennial.

GROUND CHERRIES

The varieties of ground cherry are many, and the selection changes every year. Some changes involve flavor profiles that claim to taste like pineapple or mango. Some are rebranded with more appealing and marketable names, like Cape gooseberry, goldenberries, or Inca berries. Although many seed catalogs refer to them as ground cherries, they are not true cherries, nor are they gooseberries; they are closer to tomatoes than to any other vegetable. Most eaters find that the majority of ground cherries taste like a sweet yet flavorless tart tomato—but when forced to be honest, many gardeners (myself included) find their flavor less exciting than their name suggests.

For decades, husk cherries were regarded as a garden novelty. But they have appeared more recently in farmers' markets and in CSA boxes. Their use in the kitchen is somewhat limited, however. They are used as garnishes at best, or for snacking while in the garden. Their flavor is odd in that they seem neither sweet enough to eat by themselves, nor tomatoey enough for use in a salad, where they seem cloyingly sweet in comparison to other raw vegetables. Still, the plants and their fruit are beautiful to some. A few plants can be tucked into a large container or into the corner of the garden. Some varieties have fruit that only ripens after it falls off the plant, so harvesting involves a daily picking off the ground and then allowing the fruit to ripen on a plate for a few days.

OPPOSITE: Look for purple to lime green tomatillo varieties, such as this 'Toma Verde'. The smaller husk berry is 'Goldie', an easy-to-grow husk cherry that will self-seed if allowed.

ABOVE LEFT: Tomatillo flowers. **ABOVE RIGHT:** 'Goldie' husk cherry. Husk cherries include a number or smaller-fruited Physalis species. Their flavor is a bit like pineapple but less sweet.

TOMATILLO

Setting husk cherries aside for a moment, the most significant and most useful *Physalis* member is the tomatillo. These can have great value for the home chef, especially if Mexican food is on the menu. Tomatillos fall under two species: *Physalis philadelphica* (green) and *P. ixocarpa* (often purple). There are multiple strains to choose from, including many selections of both dark-skinned and green varieties hailing from specific regions in Central America and Mexico.

TOMATILLO CULTURE

Like tomatoes, tomatillos (and ground cherries) are primarily warm-weather crops. Seeds can be started indoors under lights or in a warm greenhouse 4 to 6 weeks before last frost. Seeds germinate best in warm soil (80°F) and appreciate bright light for at least 14 hours a day. They handle transplanting without sulking. Set plants outside in a large pot or on the ground to harden off for a week before final planting. Staking or trellising is needed, as the plants can be wildly rampant. Keeping stems off the ground will keep them from rooting wherever they touch.

Tomatillos are vigorous growers when provided with rich, loamy soil and moisture. Plant more than just one plant, as a single plant in the garden will rarely set fruit. Tomatillo harvests increase significantly with more than one pollinator in the pack.

PESTS AND DISEASE

Tomatillos are vulnerable to most of the same diseases as tomatoes and peppers, but they are more resistant. The most common pest is the tomato fruitworm (*Helicoverpa zea*), more commonly known as the corn earworm. This pest sometimes goes unnoticed until you harvest the fruit and see tiny holes made by the larvae. In summer, once the eggs hatch, the small white larvae burrow into the fruit, where they feed and mature. Once the fruit is cut open, brown areas of decay and feces often reveal the culprit. The safest way to control these pests is to check for eggs or damage. The eggs are laid both on the top surfaces of leaves and on the bottom. White at first, they'll turn brownish or tan just before the hatch. If the eggs are black, don't worry about them—they are a favorite of a parasitic wasp, and these eggs have already been destroyed by more beneficial larvae. Control significant outbreaks with *Bacillus thuringiensis*, but in most home garden situations, a few rotten tomatoes (or tomatillos) aren't a problem.

Flea beetles can be problematic as well, but mostly in damaging the foliage. They may make tiny holes in the leaves and the husks, but they rarely damage the fruit. Powdery mildew can become a problem in late summer if grown under close conditions. An organic fungicide can be used if necessary.

HARVEST

Pick tomatillos when the fruit has filled or torn through the husk. Depending on the variety, the fruit may turn dark purple, or it may remain green, but with a pale-yellow blush. A sticky substance on the fruit is normal but should be washed off before using the fruit in a recipe.

VARIETIES

GROUND CHERRIES

'Goldie' open-pollinated (75 days)—The old-fashioned ground cherry with golden-yellow fruit in small, straw-colored husks. Fruits often drop before ripening. Pick up and bring indoors to ripen on a plate.

TOMATILLOS

'Toma Verde' open-pollinated (60 days)—A light-green tomatillo with large fruit and a flatter shape. Similar to those found in specialty Mexican markets.

'De Milpa' open-pollinated (70 days)—An heirloom variety found in Mexico and often favored by many home cooks. A bit later to mature. Color is green with a violet blush.

'Amarylla' open-pollinated (70 days)—A bright-yellow heirloom with smaller fruit. Its flavor resembles that of a ground cherry, and it can be eaten raw or used in making sweeter salsa.

'Tiny from Coban' open-pollinated (70 days)—A variety collected in Mexico by Jere Gettle of Baker Creek Heirloom Seeds. It is small like a ground cherry but has dark-violet fruit about the size of a dime.

Tomatillo husks look like their close relatives the old-fashioned Japanese lanterns, but these husks never turn red. Wait for the fruit to mature, when the fruits enlarge and split through the sides of the husks, but before the fruits split themselves.

MELONS, CUCUMBERS, SQUASH, AND GOURDS

At first glance, the crops lumped together in this chapter may seem like a grab bag of miscellaneous vegetables thrown together near the end of the book because they did not fit in any other category. This is actually not the case. Melons, cucumbers, squash, and gourds are all part of the same important family—the cucurbits. The individual genuses come from different parts of the world, and their fruits may not resemble one another very closely, but they do have some common traits. For instance, they are all vining plants that produce male and female flowers. When the female flower is pollinated by the male flower, fruit forms at the base of the female flower and eventually turns into the mature vegetable.

The cucurbits represent some of the most productive and largest vegetables known to gardens. You will find a wide range of days to maturity in the family, but all members grow best in rich, fertile soil, and all are heavy feeders that require ample amounts of water supplied very consistently. But the best quality that cucurbits share is that, among all vegetables, these are the most fun to grow and harvest.

MELONS

Among all the Cucurbitaceae family, the melon reigns supreme. Unlike other family members, it evolved from a primitive species native to Africa, whereas the rest of the family grew up in South America. Their early introduction into the Middle East, the Mediterranean, and eventually Europe made melons one of the first crops to be domesticated in both the Old World and the New World.

In many home gardens today, melons are a little-valued crop. It's not that home gardeners don't want to grow melons, but rather that they appear too challenging or too sprawling for a small area.

Melons are, however, very rewarding when grown well. Even in cold climates, many accomplished gardeners can grow watermelons. As with any new venture, expect a few failures at first, but learn from your errors and adjust techniques and approaches.

Growing melons is not as simple as some pop-a-seed-into-the-ground-and-forget-about-it crops, but they are completely feasible, even in small gardens. It is a mistake, however, to generalize about melons, because there are so many types, each with their own needs and preferred environment. Of all the cucurbits, melons are probably the most demanding when it comes to siting. They love full days of sunshine, rich soil, and a nice breeze to dry their foliage. A few good pollinators are always a bonus.

VARIETY MATTERS

Some melons are gigantic and aggressive, others are pocket-sized and a bit timid. Making a wise choice of variety is especially important with melons. It requires a little restraint, as there are so many delicious and beautiful melons to choose from, especially in the heirloom seed catalogs. First, make a wish list (this is the fun part), and then factor in your growing conditions as they compare to each melon's needs. If you want to try a giant watermelon, then by all means try it, but be sure you are prepared to offer it what it needs—lots of space, fertility, and warmth, an extended season, and plenty of water. Edit your choices based on days to maturity and your garden's size.

START SEEDS EARLY

As warm-weather plants, all melons benefit from an early start in individual cell containers at least 3 inches in diameter. You can shorten the outdoor growing time of the longest-season melons by starting them under lights, but this is not ideal

OPPOSITE: Homegrown watermelon is a dream for many, but it is completely possible, even in a small space. Stick to the smaller icebox-sized melons for the best results, especially in the north. 'Sugar Baby' is the go-to standard for small, red watermelons that are easy for the home gardener, while 'Sunshine' F1 is a fine, small, yellow-fleshed watermelon so delicious that it will transform your opinion about seeded watermelon.

MASTERING TECHNIQUES

- Choose early-maturing varieties in colder climates.
- Start seeds early in pots where it's warm to gain a few weeks.
- Enrich soil to ensure the highest fertility possible.
- Use a black plastic mulch to keep weeds down and soil warm.
- Use a floating row cover to create a microclimate of warmth in spring.
- Make sure melons get a steady supply of water.
- Only allow one or two melons to form on each vine.
- Choose a planting site with full sun.
- Monitor for pollinators or hand-pollinate if bees seem scarce.

due to the low light quality most units present. A warm greenhouse is a better place to start melon seeds early, as both light quality and day length are factors in creating a healthy plant. Because few gardeners have such a luxury, you can try sowing seeds indoors a few weeks earlier in individual cells that you've filled with the best-quality sterile potting mix. But set the trays outside on warm days where they can get at least partial sun, as subjecting plants to the brightest light is helpful. I often sow seed in cells outdoors just as the weather turns warm. The natural breezes and outdoor exposure will strengthen them, and they'll grow rapidly if the weather warms. Full sunshine is ideal. Keep an eye on watering, and when cool weather threatens, bring the pots indoors to a warm, bright location for a few days, but return them outside as soon as you can. Monitor pots to see if roots are beginning to emerge, and repot if necessary with minimal root handling. Slip a rootball out carefully and set it into another pot without disturbing the soil.

If your garden soil is above 70°F, seeds can be sown directly into the bed.

PREPARING MELON BEDS

Plant your melons in the sunniest spot in your garden. At a very minimum, it should get at least 6 to 8 hours of direct sunlight, or the melons will mature slowly and not set fruit well.

The importance of fertility cannot be overemphasized. The greatest success will come from beds where the soil has been prepared with additional organic material, such as aged manure, as well as organic or inorganic fertilizer. If using plastic sheet mulch, be sure to dig-in fertilizer before laying the mulch over the bed in the spring. If you happen to keep chickens, spread the coop-dressing over the bed throughout the winter and turn it in as soon as the ground can be tilled in the early spring. Farmers dig-in aged manure to a depth of 24 inches, which may seem excessive, but most melons have very deep roots, especially cantaloupes. Underfed melons will be small and inferior. If you have issues with using fertilizer or manure, you're probably better off skipping melons.

WATERING AND MULCHING

All melons, particularly watermelons, need plenty of water. Irrigation of some sort must be provided. In water-scarce areas, set up an efficient drip-hose system. You should always avoid sprinkling, since water on the foliage can bring on a variety of ailments—such as powdery mildew—in late summer. Avoid early outbreaks by watering in the morning and only on bright, sunny days if you are broadcasting water overhead.

Mulch will help significantly in retaining water. The use of a synthetic mulch such as black sheet plastic

OPPOSITE: The fancy French 'Charentais' melons are small and perfect for those who are seeking a luxury in late summer. In so many ways, this is our favorite.

FROM LEFT TO RIGHT: 'Delice de la Table' French heirloom melon, 'Charentais' melon, 'Golden Honeymoon' honeydew.

offers many advantages, beginning with weed suppression and its ability to heat the soil early in the year. Row covers have reinvented melon culture and made it a cold-climate possibility. Plan on at least 100 square feet of garden space for giant watermelon varieties. You can use a square 10 x 10-foot layout, or stake down plastic over raised hills or rows that are 3 to 4 feet wide and run as long as you can make them. Use earth staples to pin down the sheeting, and tuck in a few rocks here and there for ballast. Some growers on larger farms have good success with porous woven weed-barrier fabric (similar to landscape fabric). It's carried by many agricultural supply stores and hardware stores in various widths and lengths, usually starting in 3-foot-wide rolls.

SETTING PLANTS INTO THE GARDEN

Once the bed is prepared and the weather has fully warmed, seedlings can be planted into the garden. Melons (except for dwarf varieties) grow larger than you may expect. Two plants can be set 8 inches apart every 3 feet. Cut the weed barrier/sheeting in an X shape at the proper spacing to provide access points for your plants. Remove a melon seedling from its pot, being careful not to damage or disturb the rootball. Water each plant in well with a good liquid balanced fertilizer (10-10-10 or similar) made to the manufacturer's directions for strength. Inorganic fertilizer is most effective for all seedlings, especially for the quick-growing melons that need quick access to nitrogen at this phase.

FERTILITY

Prepare the entire bed with well-composted manure (the type that comes in a bag from the nursery will do). A sprinkling of a balanced granular feed is helpful to start, but will last only so long, as melons are robust and hungry growers. A second hit of nitrogen is beneficial about 3 weeks after planting, especially if the plants are established and growing lushly by midsummer. Once female flowers form, cut back on the nitrogen and switch to a 2-8-8 ration every 3 weeks to refocus the plants on creating flowers and large fruit. As always, keep an eye on moisture level, and water deeply.

PRUNING VINES

All melons benefit from some control. A reason why many fail or yield small melons is that their vines were not pruned. Just after fruit set in midsummer, walk through the beds attentively and cut off all excess fruit so the plant can focus on supplying its limited resources to the chosen few winners. With the larger watermelons, leave only one fruit per vine. Cantaloupes should be cut back to four melons per vine, or maybe five if the soil is rich and the water supply is ample and consistent.

DISEASES AND PESTS

To avoid the common diseases of Fusarium and nematodes, practice crop rotation—it is the only alternative to chemical insecticides. Most home gardeners won't experience many other problems, except powdery mildew in the late summer. To discourage that, and other fungus and mildew, avoid watering in the afternoon or evening.

Slugs can be a problem in some areas, and these are best dealt with by applying diatomaceous earth near the stems or as a ring around the fruits if they are sitting on plastic mulch.

Sunscald can often be a problem if the foliage isn't large enough to shade the fruit, or if the fruit is growing too large. Some growers improvise by creating mini sun-screens out of row-cover fabric, or by making little homemade tents or umbrellas, but this is rather extreme. Instead, you can carefully lift the fruit and vine and reposition the fruit so the foliage covers it.

HARVESTING MELONS

It is not always easy to ascertain when melons are ready to pick. The popular advice is to smell a melon or tap it to see if it sounds hollow. This is often confusing, or just plain incorrect. Ripeness depends on the type of melon, and there is no single indicator that is reliable other than trial-and-error experience.

MELON TYPES, VARIETIES, AND GROUPS

The term "melon" itself can be confusing, but most gardeners agree that it refers to those melons within *Cucumis* (the cucumber genus) and *Citrullus* (the watermelon genus). There are others that fit the description, though, such as Asian gourds like bitter melons (*Momordica*). But for the purposes of this book I've divided those into their own separate section.

Muskmelons and Cantaloupes. Muskmelons and cantaloupes (and most melons included in the Reticulatus group) are the easiest when it comes to judging ripeness. They will emit a lovely melon fragrance when ripe, and many change color. In fact, these are the easiest melons to grow as well, so they are great for beginners and for those gardening in short growing seasons. These melons all share some physical characteristics, such as the netted (reticulated) skin that develops on many of these varieties.

Honeydews, Casabas, and Crenshaws. Things get a bit more challenging with more tropical melons such as casabas, crenshaws, and honeydews (the Inodorus group). The name "Inodorus" references the fact that all have little to no odor when ripe. Occasionally you may have to sacrifice a fruit because you are tricked into picking it underripe. I've found that it helps if I apply slight pressure to the blossom end with my thumb to

LEFT: 'Tigger' has a better name than it tastes—it's best more as a novelty than as a fruit. RIGHT: 'Schoon's Hardshell' is a New York State heirloom and a favorite of many melon experts. It has hard skin but a luscious salmon-colored flesh. OPPOSITE: 'Carolina Cross' watermelon.

see if it gives, especially if I've been watching the melon mature. Even a slight fragrance tells me it's ready.

The Inodorus group includes some of the most luscious tropical melons. If I can get them out into my garden early enough, there is a chance I'll get a superior crop, although I know that in some years the crop will be disappointing due to cool weather. Imperfect conditions can cause them to be too seedy when picked, but few melons compare to the delicious Inodorus specimens such as the Santa Claus melon, or the pineapple tart flavor of the giant and impressive Banana melon.

Watermelons. Judging the ripeness of watermelons is challenging. Of all the melons, they typically take the longest to ripen. In cold-climate gardens, they often are not ready for picking until the very end of summer as first frost approaches. Smaller watermelons like 'Sugar Baby' are easiest, and their small vines mean you can grow them in containers if you wish. Some say that the stem end will begin to darken or dry as ripeness is achieved, but I've found

that a good guess is usually right. As watermelons mature in your garden, you build a relationship with them, and it becomes almost instinctual to know which are ripe.

Other Melon Types. With the advent of heirloom seed catalogs and seed exchanges, there seems to be an endless parade of newly available, gorgeous melons arriving on the scene. Many are forgotten old varieties, and others are regional specialties that were once popular in the Victorian era but now are novelties. All are worth growing for one reason or another, but be prepared for some beauties that may have some drawbacks, based on contemporary standards. For example, heirloom growers have flocked to the tiny tiger or pocket melons, which are as colorful as ornamental gourds but too small and flavorless (in my opinion) to have much value other than as a conversation piece.

Some new stars are worth growing, however, particularly the Ha'Ogen types sometimes referred to as Israeli melons, and many French heirlooms that are popular with fine chefs, such as the 'Charentais' types.

CUCUMBERS

Cucumis sativus

Cucumbers are ancient in comparison to some other cucurbits. Around in the time of the early Romans and Greeks, they are true biblical fruits. The early Spanish explorers brought the cucumber to North America, where the genus was quickly adopted into the diets of indigenous Americans and then European colonists.

Some cultures, particularly in Asia, allowed cucumbers to ripen like melons. Some ancient varieties had reticulated skins of maroon, or brown skins with brilliant golden-yellow accents. Many cucumbers of this type are still preferred in areas such as Bhutan and Sikkim. With the seeds removed, they are braised and cooked like Asian winter melons.

Today, cucumber varieties are numerous, and their forms range from the tiniest French cornichon to giant Sikkim brown cucumbers. While there are some novelties, they remain viewed as a culinary vegetable of three primary types: long, green slicers; American picklers; and the English seedless or popular "baby" cucumbers, which are raised in greenhouses.

POLLINATION

As with most cucurbits, cucumbers sometimes need help being pollinated, and most are considered monoecious. Some are gynoecious (varieties that produce all-female flowers), so they must be planted in proximity to a variety that produces male flowers to be able to set fruit. Their fruit production is very high as a result, but most are commercial varieties only. Some cucumber varieties are parthenocarpic, meaning they do not require any pollinator. These are ideal for culture in greenhouses or hoop houses.

CULTURE

Cucumbers are warm-weather crops, germinating best after the soil has warmed to at least 70°F. You can get a jump on the season by starting seeds in pots, but keep them outdoors on warm, sunny days. Sow two or three seeds into individual pots or 3-inch cell containers. Use sterile, soilless mix. Seeds should be sown ½ inch deep, and the soil needs to be kept warm (above 70°F). In fact, cucumber seeds won't germinate if the soil temperatures dip below 50°F. Transplant young plants directly into prepared beds just as the first true leaf appears. Be careful not to disturb the rootball, but two to three seedlings per rootball is okay.

Cucumber beds should be prepared well in advance of planting. Dig-in rich composted organic material as well as aged manure. Cucumbers demand high fertility. If testing, cucumbers grow best in a soil with a pH of 6.8 to 7.2.

Moisture is key for cucumbers, and any drought will affect the yield significantly by causing blossom abortion and low fruiting. Black plastic sheet mulch will aid in discouraging weeds and keeping the soil warm and moist. Water in the morning during dry spells, especially when the plants are flowering and fruiting to reduce the risk of encouraging powdery mildew.

PESTS AND DISEASE

The most troublesome pest for cucumber growers is the cucumber beetle, although it is less problematic for newer hybrids that have been bred to not produce a certain bitter compound that attracts the beetle. Row covers will help discourage egg-laying females and transient pests from neighboring gardens. Some growers build a cagelike structure over their beds and staple floating row cover material over it if cucumber beetles become a problem. Attempting to handpick beetles is unrealistic and often not effective in controlling the problem.

If you live in a humid climate, powdery mildew will eventually take your cucumber crop. First appearing as whitish, dusty spots on the foliage, the fungal disease will inevitably spread to make each leaf look as if it were dipped in a grayish powder. It's more common later in the summer, and one can discourage or delay outbreaks by watering early and only on sunny days. Once cucumbers start bearing, you must visit the patch daily to keep up with the harvest. Mature fruit will turn yellow, and while still edible (even preferred in some cultures), the younger cucumber is best for fresh dishes.

Good practices to follow are generally the same as for other powdery mildew–susceptible crops such as tomatoes, squashes, and peppers: annual crop rotation, impeccable cleanliness (burning old vines and not composting them, even washing one's hands between touching plants), and selecting disease-resistant hybrids over heirlooms. Bacterial wilt is more serious but as it is spread by insects, the use of a floating row cover over a structure may be the most effective prevention method for home gardeners.

TYPES AND VARIETIES

Commercially, cucumbers are organized by type, which is determined more by their shape than by usage. A commercial catalog may list a variety named 'Socrates' that is described as a large 'Beit Alpha'-type. Often the names of old or popular varieties are used both as the name of a type as well as a varietal name, so while you may see a new variety listed as a 'Kirby'-type, you may also find a plant tag at a nursery that may simply say 'Kirby'. It can be confusing, but retailers know that most consumers know vegetables by their most common name or type. Catalogs and nurseries that service home gardeners tend to categorize the cucumber offerings mostly by usage. For example: pickling, salad, slicing, greenhouse, and burpless. Taking the extra time to research, learn, and attempt to grow the many named varieties of vegetables is both educational and fun for home gardeners, and is one of the great benefits of growing a home vegetable garden.

Slicing Cucumbers. Also known as American slicing, these are the standard large, zucchini-shaped cucumbers often sold with a waxy coating on the skin. The most common type in North America, slicers include varieties like the open-pollinated 'Marketmore' series.

OPPOSITE: At maturity, many varieties of heirloom cucumbers often turn red or golden yellow, or have beautifully netted or reticulated skins. Many are staples of tribal areas in Thailand, Burma, and Laos, and I've seen them hanging in gardens throughout Yunnan and Tibet, where their mild, crispy flesh is preferred over the immature cucumbers the rest of the world enjoys.

Pickling Cucumbers. Sometimes referred to as European pickling cucumbers, these smaller cucumbers are lighter green with spines, and include the gherkins. Picked very small, some varieties are pickled without sugar in France and are known as cornichons. Despite being labeled as "pickling," these cucumbers are delicious fresh, especially when immature. Mature fruit will turn golden-yellow, and while they may still be consumed raw or cooked, they first need to be peeled and seeded.

Burpless, Asian, or English Cucumbers. This group includes the most popular cucumbers today, often with regional names and distinctions. All are thin-skinned baby types, usually raised in greenhouses, though they can certainly be raised outdoors. Longer-fruited varieties are best trellised, while baby types are better under glass. 'Beit Alpha' types are a popular class of thin-skinned cucumbers that aren't really all that new. First introduced in the 1930s and named for a kibbutz in northern Israel where they were bred (by Hanka Lazarson), we are starting to see 'Beit Alpha' types sold in seed catalogs. You may see them sold both as an heirloom (the open-pollinated variety simply named 'Beit Alpha') and as a hybrid bred for greenhouses. Either is excellent in the garden. The hybrid seed is more expensive, but the cucumber fruit is pure perfection and the plants are high-producing, as most are gynoecious. 'Beit Alpha' types are parthenocarpic, a fancy name for a plant that produces asexual flowers.

The fruit of the burpless cucumber is virtually seedless, which explains the high cost of seed as well as the fact that these types now dominate the market. While originally bred for commercial culture in greenhouses, more and more seed catalogs are carrying them.

Familiar terms for thin-skinned cucumbers are Persian, Lebanese, or Armenian—all often sold as "Middle Eastern" types. Fancier heirlooms are also becoming popular but are often grown more as a novelty than for fresh eating. The kekiri from India and Nepal, while popular in its native countries, is often grown in the West just for its gourdlike appearance. But they are delicious cooked in curries or even eaten raw when immature.

TOP: The classic 'Boston Pickling' cucumber. **BOTTOM:** 'Sikkim', an Asian cucumber variety.

VARIETIES

There are hundreds of varieties of cucumbers. Here are a few standouts:

SLICING TYPES

'Corinto' F1 hybrid (48 days)—Early slicer with 7- to 8-inch fruit. Highly productive as it is both gynoecious and parthenocarpic.

'Marketmore 97' open-pollinated (60 days)—Sets the standard among the slicing types. The Marketmore series consists of many varieties followed by the year each was developed. Marketmore 97 is exceptionally disease-resistant and thus a good choice for organic growers. It even shows resistance to the cucumber beetle.

PICKLING TYPES

'Northern Pickling' open-pollinated (48 days)—One of the very best pickling types. Black spines on pale-green fruits. A heavy bearer that is great for dill pickles.

'Adam Gherkin' F1 hybrid (47 days)—A high-end market gherkin that can now be raised in the home garden. High-performing (it is both gynoecious and parthenocarpic), it's more disease-resistant than earlier gherkin types. Pick while very small (2 to 3 inches) for traditional gherkins, or smaller for true cornichon pickles.

'H-19' open-pollinated (57 days)—Known as a little-leaf type, 'H-19' is productive, disease-resistant, and parthenocarpic. It branches more than other varieties, but its real offering is that it forms leaves that are half the size of other types (if you've ever spent hours hunting for hidden cucumbers, this is your variety).

ENGLISH/SEEDLESS/BURPLESS TYPES

'Socrates' F1 hybrid (52 days)—7- to 8-inch high-quality fruit said to have the best flavor of all the 'Beit Alpha' types. Parthenocarpic, it can handle low temperatures near 50°F for short periods.

'Diva' (58 days)—Tender and seedless cucumber for greenhouses or gardens. Best picked small for baby cukes. 2002 AAS winner.

'Suyo Long' open-pollinated (61 days)—Traditional Asian cucumber. Sweet, ribbed fruit best raised on a trellis to keep the fruits straight.

NOVELTY CUCUMBERS

'Lemon Cuke' open-pollinated (65 days)—A round cucumber that looks like a lemon. Crispy flesh and tender, pale-yellow skin. Popular at farmers' markets and with kids, it is good for pickling. A late-maturing variety.

'Sikkim' (50–75 days)—An ancient cucumber grown in the eastern Himalayas. It is similar to other Asian brown cucumbers such as 'Gagon' and 'Poona Kheera'. The first Westerner to collect these was the famed Sir Joseph Hooker in 1848. The dark, rust-colored fruit looks like a pickling cuke when immature, but turns golden with a reticulated skin like a cantaloupe when ripe. The internal flesh is edible if peeled and seeded.

'Mexican Sour Gherkin' open-pollinated (67 days)—Not botanically from the same genus as the cucumber, it's from the genus *Melothria*, but still within Cucurbitaceae. Similar in flavor to cucumbers, most people grow it for its utter cuteness. They look like tiny watermelons, thus earning the alternate names "cucamelons" or "mouse melons." The vines are long, and they demand more heat than other cucumbers. Start seeds indoors a few weeks early with bottom heat. Often too seedy to really enjoy eating, pick them very small (under 1 inch) for fewer seeds if using in a recipe.

SUMMER SQUASH

Cucurbita pepo

ZUCCHINI, SUMMER, AND SCALLOP SQUASH

As far as common vegetables go, the summer squash is a relative newcomer in the West. Before 1900, few people outside of the Mediterranean grew summer squash. In Italy, of course, summer squash has a long history, but it wasn't until the early twentieth century that these vegetables made it to the United States, first arriving in 1918 as "Italian squash." Without a doubt, the summer squash roost is ruled by the zucchini.

Summer squash are organized by botanists into two groups: the Vegetable Marrow group and the Cocozelle group. Lovers of summer squash know the difference, for a young, tender Cocozelle remains firmer and tastes nuttier. Other groups exist in the summer squash clan. These are the scallop group and the well-known crookneck and straightneck groups both native to North America. The crookneck and straightneck summer squashes are lovely yellow fruits that grow, as in most of these groups, on non-vining plants. This makes them convenient for the smaller home garden, although some of these bush varieties can grow rather large.

All members of the summer squash clan love a similar culture of rich, loamy soil, excellent fertility, warm temperatures, and constant moisture. They are well known as easy, even fun, to grow. High-yielding when planted in full sun, the plants only suffer if they receive too much shade or are planted close together. These thin-skinned summer squashes are best when picked very immature. The blossoms are edible and enjoyed as a delicacy, often stuffed with rich, creamy cheeses and fried. Pick open flowers early in the morning, choosing either all male, as they will come earlier in the season, or female ones with the small immature fruit still attached.

CULTURE

All summer squash share a similar culture. Each has seeds that will germinate quickly in warm soil (temperatures near 70°F). Seeds can be sown directly in open soil or started in cell containers outdoors and then transplanted into prepared beds a few weeks later. Sow two or three seeds into each cell, ½ inch deep, in a sterile potting mix. As with all cucurbits, cleanliness is key to avoid spreading any pathogens. After seedlings emerge, remove the weakest ones when setting out plants, in order to allow the strongest one adequate space to develop. Avoid disturbing the rootball by carefully unpotting each seedling and setting it into a prepared hole.

Beds should be prepared using plastic mulch or weed-suppressing fabric to help keep the soil warm and consistently moist during irregular rainfall periods. Water is important, but water on the leaves can encourage earlier outbreaks of powdery mildew. Water early in the morning, preferably on breezy, sunny days.

OPPOSITE: The variety of summer squash available today goes way beyond zucchini and yellow crookneck.

VARIETIES

ZUCCHINI GROUP

No need to introduce most gardeners to zucchini. Tender and flavorful, it is rarely used as a mature vegetable, with most preferring the immature fruit.

Cocozelle (Costata) type—The firmer, ribbed gourds known collectively as the Cocozelle types look like striped or ribbed zucchini. While farm stands or CSAs may refer to them as zucchini, Cocozelle is indeed a unique group. Taste one and you'll know instantly. Their texture is firmer (never mushy), and they are often the secret crop of in-the-know horticulturists and gardeners.

'Costata Romanesco' open-pollinated (52 days)—A market variety from Italy. Many growers will agree that this is the finest-tasting summer squash.

'Flaminio' F1 hybrid (50 days)—An improved Costata-type hybrid with all the characteristics of the heirloom 'Costata Romanesco', but with higher yields and a less sprawling bush.

'Striato d'Italia' open-pollinated (58 days)—A beautiful Cocozelle-type summer squash with stripes that alternate from light green to dark green. Best when picked while young.

'Reward' F1 hybrid (49 days)—High-yielding, classic all-green zucchini with high resistance to powdery mildew and other diseases.

'Goldmine' F1 hybrid (52 days)—A new yellow zucchini with pale-yellow stripes.

'Green Tiger' F1 hybrid (50 days)—An attractive green-striped zucchini good for farmers' markets and home gardens. Best if harvested before 7 inches in length.

CROOKNECKS AND STRAIGHTNECKS

The familiar yellow summer squash comes in two types, crookneck and straightneck. While both were developed independently by back-breeding, there are dozens of varieties of each.

'Multipik' F1 hybrid (50 days)—Improved yellow straightneck variety recommended for high performance and yields.

'Gold Star' F1 hybrid (50 days)—An improved smooth-skinned yellow crookneck with excellent disease resistance.

SCALLOP GROUP

'Sunburst' F1 hybrid (52 days)—A bright, golden yellow pattypan that is excellent when picked at "baby" size as well as at 3 inches. A 1985 AAS winner.

'Y-Star' F1 hybrid (50 days)—A yellow pattypan with a larger green disk at the blossom end. Prolific and adaptable to many soil conditions.

'Bennings Green Tint' heirloom (52 days)—An all-green pattypan that is best when picked small (2 to 3 inches in diameter).

KOUSA or VEGETABLE MARROW GROUP

'Magda' F1 hybrid (48 days)—A new Kousa-type variety with smooth, pale-green skin and a texture that makes the Middle Eastern varieties so favored by home cooks. Great for stuffing as they hold their shape, and prized for their nutty flavor when prepared like zucchini.

MIXED HYBRIDS

'Zephyr' F1 hybrid (54 days)—A 1999 introduction from Johnny's Selected Seeds that was the result of a cross between a yellow crookneck and a yellow acorn squash. The results are a phenomenal visual treat—fruits are shaped like a yellow straightneck but look as if they were dipped into green dye on one end.

MASTERING TECHNIQUES
TIPS FOR GROWING SUMMER SQUASH

- Make sure the plants have heat, rich soil, and plenty of water.
- The use of black plastic mulch warms the soil and helps maintain steady moisture.
- Newer varieties are better-performing and more disease-resistant.
- Space at 4 feet apart. Few fruits will form if plants are set too close together.
- Fruit decay starting at the blossom end (blossom-end rot) is caused by calcium deficiency brought on by drought, so maintain constant soil moisture so plants can access calcium.

TOP: 'Lebanese' white bush marrow, or 'Kousa' squash. **MIDDLE:** 'Costata Romanesco'. **BOTTOM:** Squash blossoms can be picked and stuffed as either female (with baby fruit attached) or as male blooms. Any squash variety will do, but summer squashes are the most tender.

WINTER SQUASH

Cucurbita maxima, C. pepo, C. moschata, and C. argyrosperma

All winter or storage squash are New World plants, and all are native to South America, but gardeners worldwide have adopted them and developed their unique selections over the past 300 years. Some are delicious and useful in the kitchen, while others are more decorative and used in autumn displays.

We thank France for its buff-skinned 'Musquée de Provence'. Also for the classic cinnabar-colored Cinderella pumpkin 'Rouge Vif d'Etampes' and for 'Galeux d'Eysines', with its pale, coral-tinted and oddly peanut-like encrusted skin. We have Australia to thank for its handsome grayish-blue 'Jarrahdale' and the beautifully ribbed 'Queensland Blue'.

Japan has brought the world plenty of squashes, but the most popular perhaps is 'Red Kuri' (also known as 'Hokkaido' or 'Baby Red Hubbard'). It is in France where 'Red Kuri' (known there as 'Potimarron') is most treasured. Parisians look for it every autumn, and chefs celebrate its arrival at the markets.

Today, many of the most colorful and oddly shaped winter squashes are grown more for decoration than for food, but don't be fooled by their sometimes ugly appearance—under their warty, beautifully colored skins lie some of the most useful vegetables you can grow in the home garden.

Winter squash are easy to grow. They are the perfect entry-level vegetable for children and first-time gardeners to try, since they grow abundantly in almost any garden when given enough space, water, sunlight, and food. However, with hundreds of varieties now available from seed, choosing the right variety to grow can be challenging.

WINTER SQUASH TYPES

Winter squash can be confusing to many, so a bit of organization will help you understand the different types. Botanists arrange all the winter squash by species, while home growers know them by variety. Knowing the exact species of squash is more important than you may think, as there are some significant differences both in how to grow and how to cook them.

Most winter squash can be organized into four species: *Cucurbita maxima*, *C. pepo*, *C. moschata*, and *C. argyrosperma*. Within each of these, ethnobotanists and taxonomists have suggested "groups" or "types" to help gardeners understand and lump together similar varieties.

Cucurbita pepo is a species with plenty of variation just within the single species itself—it contains both winter storage squashes and summer squashes, the most familiar being the yellow summer squashes and the zucchinis. What most people don't know is that the common orange pumpkin is also included in the same species (*C. pepo* var. *pepo*), as are spaghetti squash (*C. pepo* var. *fastiga-*

ta) and acorn squash (*C. pepo* var. *turbinata*). All *Cucurbita pepo* share some characteristics, whether they are picked immature or kept on the vine to mature into a storage squash. Members of this species have thin skin, and they tend to be fibrous, less sweet, and more watery.

Squash in the species *C. maxima* are the most flavorful and colorful of all squash varieties (and there are plenty to choose from—over 350). *C. maxima* varieties are some of the most beloved of winter squashes and include many of the striking and oddly shaped heirlooms found at farm stands—the giant blue hubbard, for example, which can grow to over 100 pounds and has gorgeous, slate-gray skin. This group also includes some of the most flavorful storage squashes—the sort that are best consumed after aging indoors for a few months. Examples include the "turbans," the many buttercup types, and 'Lakota', a glorious coral and green squash said to have been selected and developed by the Lakota tribe in North America.

The third group of winter squashes is *C. moschata*—a group that contains the fewest varieties, but some of the most versatile and flavorful in the kitchen. While the group contains rarely seen varieties like 'Cheese Pumpkin', 'Seminole', and the long 'Tromboncino', it also contains the most familiar of all winter squashes: the butternut. Butternuts are unique—neither fibrous nor watery nor dry, they are the perfect balance of texture, flavor, and color. Developed in Waltham, Massachusetts, in the 1940s, it quickly became the standard by which all squash is measured. With brilliant-orange flesh and easy-to-peel skin, it remains one of North America's favorite squashes.

HOW TO GROW WINTER SQUASH

All cucurbits love warm, rich soil, consistent moisture, and sunny weather. Winter squash seeds can vary between large and surprisingly small. Most are big and easy to sow, however, and they can be planted directly into the soil once it has warmed to 65°F, or started in 3-inch pots. Sow one or two seeds per pot filled with soilless potting mix. Label each pot, as cucurbits all look the same until they fruit. Water well, and set the pots in a warm and sunny place outdoors. The large seeds will germinate quickly in the warm late-spring sunshine.

Do not attempt to sow any squash until after the weather has fully warmed up—once the leaves are fully formed on the native deciduous trees is a good timing tip. Pot-raised seedlings should be set into the prepared beds as soon as the first true leaf has formed (about a week and a half after the first two oval cotyledons have emerged).

Prepare the beds by tilling or hand-digging the soil to a depth of 12 inches, turning in plenty of organic matter and ideally lots of aged manure. Other choices for soil enrichment are a sidedressing of balanced granular feed (20-20-20) or a comparable organic feed. All squashes are heavy feeders, and a monthly sidedressing of granular feed will be helpful.

The planting site should receive 6 hours or more of direct sunlight to ensure good fruit set and maturity. Square footage is important to consider as well, for a large winter squash vine can occupy 100 square feet or more of garden space. Some growers allow their vines to just grow out over the lawn, while others try to be innovative with growing structures, but rarely do support systems work well with the larger squashes.

Winter squash is a crop for large gardens, but some bush or semi-bush varieties bred for short vines are still valuable to those with limited space. Yields will be lower, but even a half-dozen butternuts or delicatas are a significant contribution to the kitchen.

It is ideal to use a porous, woven landscape fabric as mulch, secured with earth staples or pins. The fabric will help heat the soil more evenly, keep weeds at bay, and protect the squash from the insect damage and decay that occur if they sit on the bare soil. Squash plants are rather low-maintenance beyond the initial setup and monthly feed. Keep an eye out for insect damage or powdery mildew, and keep the plot well-watered (it's best to water well in the morning on sunny days so that the foliage can dry out).

POLLINATION

Squash are considered monoecious (see page 251). While the plants can pollinate themselves, they rely on flying insects to do the task for them, but human help is often welcome (and is essential if raising plants in a greenhouse). Choose a male flower (with pollen) and rub it against a flower with a little squash (or ovary) at the end of the blossom.

HARVESTING, CURING, AND STORING

Harvesting squash can be intimidating, but there is little skill required, as the goal is to pick squash when it is fully ripe, and this happens just as the vines are naturally dying back in the autumn. Use a sharp knife or clippers to remove the stem from the plant, leaving just enough of the stem to function as an elegant decorative handle—but never attempt to lift a squash by the stem.

Winter squash is not a vegetable you should eat immediately after picking. Most benefit greatly from a period of curing indoors. This will harden their skins, increase their sugar content, and create a better texture. Winter squash must be picked just as the foliage fades, or before a very hard freeze (below 26°F), and then cured in a cool,

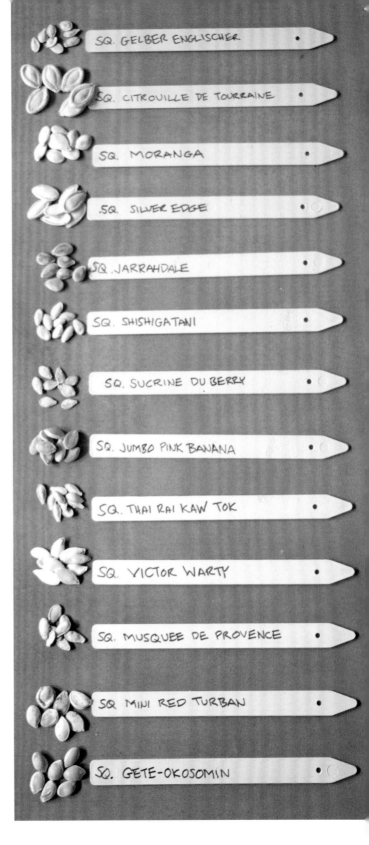

TOP LEFT: 'Speckled Hound'. **TOP MIDDLE:** 'Chicago Warted Hubbard'. **TOP RIGHT:** 'Galeux D'Eysines'. **BOTTOM LEFT:** 'Patisson Strie Melange'. **BOTTOM MIDDLE:** 'Shishigatani'. **BOTTOM RIGHT:** 'Red Kuri' or 'Potimarron'.

dry place. Vegetable historian and author Amy Goldman Fowler (author of the book *The Compleat Squash—A Passionate Grower's Guide to Pumpkins, Squashes, and Gourds*) suggests that all winter squash should be washed before curing with a 10 percent chlorine bleach solution to reduce surface contaminants. Curing temperature is not as important as relative humidity. Amy also mentions that while some growers cure squash in higher temperatures (80°F to 85°F), the higher heat also reduces long-term shelf life by evaporating some of the stored moisture. The ideal temperature is significantly cooler, between 50°F and 60°F, with moderate humidity around 60 percent. If stored too long or at higher temperatures, winter squash will begin to spoil.

VARIETIES

Cucurbita pepo group—Includes the common pumpkins, ornamental gourds, acorn squashes, scallops, zucchinis, and yellow summer squashes.

Scallop group—While most cucurbits are delicious when picked immature (think of zucchini and summer squash), those in the Scallop group are particularly tender when young, which is how most people eat them.

CUCURBITA MAXIMA

By far the most striking and visually diverse cucurbits belong to *C. maxima*. The most common groups are the Australian Blue Rind types, the Hubbard types, the Turban types, the Buttercup types, and the Exhibition squashes.

Australian Blue Rind types—Australian squashes are some of the most interesting heirloom varieties found in seed banks and heirloom seed catalogs. All have blue or grayish-green skin. Varieties include 'Triamble', 'Queensland Blue', 'Jarrahdale', and 'Crown Prince' or 'Crown Pumpkin'.

Buttercup types—The Buttercup type was first introduced in the late 1920s by Albert Yeager, who worked at the North Dakota Agricultural Experiment Station. The fruit is dry-fleshed and delicious. I find it to be the perfect squash—it is my first choice for flavor and creaminess. Some may find that its dry texture requires too much butter to make it palatable though.

Hubbard types—Arguably the most magnificent of all squash, the Hubbards are all beautiful, in colors that range from granite to sage and cinnabar to vermillion. Some are lumpy and warty, and others are just waxy. All are large, if not massive. The choicest variety may be the French 'Potimarron', or perhaps 'Red Kuri', a red Hubbard that came from Japan.

CUCURBITA PEPO GROUPS

Delicata squash—Colorful as ornamental gourds, their skins have a lovely nutty flavor and bright colors if left on for roasting.

Acorn squash—Everyone is familiar with the acorn squashes. There are many varieties, from the familiar dark-green acorns to new colors like yellow, orange, or ivory.

Spaghetti squash—Botanically, it is more closely related to summer squash, but this one is special when harvested as a winter storage squash.

CUCURBITA MOSCASTA GROUPS

Cheese pumpkins—Beautiful tan pumpkins are challenging to grow in colder climates, and are best for moderate to warm environments.

Necked squashes—Most commonly known as the Butternut varieties, these include some unusual old-timers, such as 'Winter Crookneck'. The Butternut strains are among the most popular squashes.

JAPONICA GROUP

Lesser-known in the West, but unique for both their flavor and beauty ('Futtsu' is perhaps my favorite, with its dinosaur-kale color and grayish bloom). The harvest of the 'Shishigatani' is practically a holiday in Japan. It is highly celebrated when it arrives in markets each autumn.

Cucurbita argyrosperma—This is where pumpkin seeds come from. Popular varieties include the 'Silver-Seed' gourd or 'Silver-Seed' pumpkin. Most have netted skin with combinations of green and white patterns, and they are quite distinctive as ornamentals.

LONG GOURD

Luffa acutangula, Momordica charantia, and others

Throughout Southeast Asia, India, and the Philippines, long gourds have traditionally been valued as summer vegetables, and many of these are beginning to appear in markets in North America, Europe, and elsewhere. It's no longer rare to spot trellises of long, dangling gourds on front porches and over backyard decks. These gourds may be the newest vegetables on the block, and it may take time to adopt them into your diet or planting scheme, but once you know how to grow and prepare them, their flavor will win you over.

I'm lumping together many of the luffa species and related Asian gourds here under the umbrella of Asian or long gourds, as there is no formal group recognized by botanists. All Asian gourds are tropical, lush-growing vines that appreciate a rich and very fertile soil, along with warm-to-hot summer temperatures and plenty of water. Some varieties can be difficult to find, but there are online sources. The large seeds can be pre-started in small pots or cells in late spring or early summer, a week or two before the outdoor soil temperature rises to above 70°F.

Each makes an attractive vine that must be grown on a trellis or arbor so the fruit can hang. This alone makes the vine worth growing, even if you never eat the fruit. The foliage provides shade on hot days, and the blossoms are striking, not to mention the hanging fruits with their high visual appeal as they turn yellow or orange. Many botanical gardens have also discovered the

MASTERING TECHNIQUES
TIPS FOR GROWING ASIAN LONG GOURDS

- Stand back—Asian gourds grow like crazy if raised on a large arbor or trellis system.
- Easy to grow, all these gourds need is warmth, long days, and plenty of food and water.
- The hardest part about raising Asian gourds is sourcing the seeds.
- After setting, remove all but one or two fruits from each vine.
- Don't plant too early—they are intolerant of cool weather.

beauty of planting a "gourd tunnel"—a long path covered with a trellis where these gourds can hang down captivatingly.

LUFFA AND SPONGE GOURDS

The genus *Luffa* has at least 10 species, and while known to have originated in Egypt, there is very little historical mention of its use either as a sponge or as a vegetable. Today many selections are popular throughout Asia. The most common variety found in seed catalogs is *Luffa cylindrica*—the species commonly grown to create luffa sponges.

As an immature fruit, it's delicious, and sure to increase in popularity stateside. Consumed raw when young, it tastes like a cucumber. When cooked it has the flavor of zucchini—albeit more earthy and interesting—with a more delicate texture. All luffa types are best picked young, no longer than 10 inches.

BITTER MELONS

Bitter melon may sound familiar to many gardeners, as the name and fruit appearance are memorable. But few outside of Asian communities have ever eaten it. Now these beautiful yet odd-looking and warty horned fruits are beginning to appear at local farmers' markets and upscale supermarkets. Botanically, bitter melon is known as *Momordica charantia,* but depending on what country it is grown in, it may be known as balsam pear, kho qua (Vietnamese), kaveli (Indian), or balsamina (Spanish). Some have smooth, ribbed skin, while others feature thorns or horns. All are edible if you remove the inner spongy core and the seeds. It is actually not bitter at all.

FUZZY OR HAIRY MELONS

Synonymous with wax gourds, ash gourds, petha (India), kundol (Philippines), mao kua (China), hearli meron (Japan), or bi dao (Vietnam, where it is also known as "festival gourd"), the fuzzy melon, *Benincasa hispida,* clearly plays a significant role in many Asian diets. Cultivated for over 2,300 years, just try to find a hairy melon in a market in the West today. Unless you live near a large Asian market, where an entire aisle may be dedicated to these gourds, they are virtually nonexistent. They are closely related to winter melon, and as such, both the young and mature fruit are eaten. Used in soups, stirfries, and stews, the flavor is mild and zucchini-like. The entire plant can be eaten—from the young shoots to the seeds, which are a popular snack in India and Southeast Asia. Some people even candy the fruit. While growing, the bright-yellow flowers add another dimension to the vines, and the palmate foliage is finer than that of any tropical houseplant.

CULTURE

All tropical gourds relish hot and humid weather. The slightest hint of frost, and the growing season is over. Seeds should be direct-sown if the soil is warmer than 70°F, or started in individual pots and carefully set out into the garden after their second set of leaves appear. Like all cucurbits, the plants will grow best with rich soil, along with a biweekly regimen of water-soluble fertilizer. Consistent moisture is essential as well, as these are water-heavy fruits. Pollination may have to be enhanced by hand or with a small paintbrush if a beehive isn't close by.

Note that white-flowered species (such as bottle gourds) experience greater pollination problems because they are night-blooming (flowers open at dusk, are generally pollinated by night beetles and moths before closing up in the morning). Hand-pollination is easy at dusk when the flowers open, performed either with a cotton swab (male pollen to female stigma) or by removing a male flower and turning it upside-down over a female flower (the one with the tiny gourd-shaped ovary attached to the flower), as the pollen will generally fall naturally from a dry blossom. This will increase the harvest if natural night pollinators are absent. Yellow blooming gourds like luffa are much easier as they are day-blooming. Because they tend to open in the morning (like cucumbers) they are less likely to have pollination problems as long as bees are present. With these plants, the male flowers will start blooming first, at least 2 weeks before female flowers start showing their baby gourd-shaped ovaries, so don't panic.

OPPOSITE TOP LEFT: 'Fuzzy Gourd', 'Jointed Gourd', or 'Mokwa'. **OPPOSITE BOTTOM LEFT:** 'India Hybrid Bitter Gourd'. **OPPOSITE RIGHT:** Bitter melons are easy to prepare. Split and scoop out the seeds and slice like a cucumber into rings, as you would zucchini.

METRIC CONVERSIONS

METRIC EQUIVALENT

	1/64	1/32	1/25	1/16	1/8	1/4	3/8	2/5	1/2	5/8	3/4	7/8	1	2	3	4	5	6	7	8	9	10	11	12	36	39.4
Inches (in.)	1/64	1/32	1/25	1/16	1/8	1/4	3/8	2/5	1/2	5/8	3/4	7/8	1	2	3	4	5	6	7	8	9	10	11	12	36	39.4
Feet (ft.)																								1	3	3 1/12
Yards (yd.)																									1	1 1/12
Millimeters (mm)	0.40	0.79	1	1.59	3.18	6.35	9.53	10	12.7	15.9	19.1	22.2	25.4	50.8	76.2	101.6	127	152	178	203	229	254	279	305	914	1,000
Centimeters (cm)							0.95	1	1.27	1.59	1.91	2.22	2.54	5.08	7.62	10.16	12.7	15.2	17.8	20.3	22.9	25.4	27.9	30.5	91.4	100
Meters (m)																								.30	.91	1.00

CONVERTING MEASUREMENTS

TO CONVERT:	TO:	MULTIPLY BY:
Inches	Millimeters	25.4
Inches	Centimeters	2.54
Feet	Meters	0.305
Yards	Meters	0.914
Miles	Kilometers	1.609
Square inches	Square centimeters	6.45
Square feet	Square meters	0.093
Square yards	Square meters	0.836
Cubic inches	Cubic centimeters	16.4
Cubic feet	Cubic meters	0.0283
Cubic yards	Cubic meters	0.765
Pints (U.S.)	Liters	0.473 (Imp. 0.568)
Quarts (U.S.)	Liters	0.946 (Imp. 1.136)
Gallons (U.S.)	Liters	3.785 (Imp. 4.546)
Ounces	Grams	28.4
Pounds	Kilograms	0.454
Tons	Metric tons	0.907

TO CONVERT:	TO:	MULTIPLY BY:
Millimeters	Inches	0.039
Centimeters	Inches	0.394
Meters	Feet	3.28
Meters	Yards	1.09
Kilometers	Miles	0.621
Square centimeters	Square inches	0.155
Square meters	Square feet	10.8
Square meters	Square yards	1.2
Cubic centimeters	Cubic inches	0.061
Cubic meters	Cubic feet	35.3
Cubic meters	Cubic yards	1.31
Liters	Pints (U.S.)	2.114 (Imp. 1.76)
Liters	Quarts (U.S.)	1.057 (Imp. 0.88)
Liters	Gallons (U.S.)	0.264 (Imp. 0.22)
Grams	Ounces	0.035
Kilograms	Pounds	2.2
Metric tons	Tons	1.1

CONVERTING TEMPERATURES

Convert degrees Fahrenheit (F) to degrees Celsius (C) by following this simple formula: Subtract 32 from the Fahrenheit temperature reading. Then mulitply that number by $5/9$. For example, 77°F - 32 = 45. 45 × $5/9$ = 25°C.

To convert degrees Celsius to degrees Fahrenheit, multiply the Celsius temperature reading by $9/5$, then add 32. For example, 25°C × $9/5$ = 45. 45 + 32 = 77°F.

FAHRENHEIT   CELSIUS

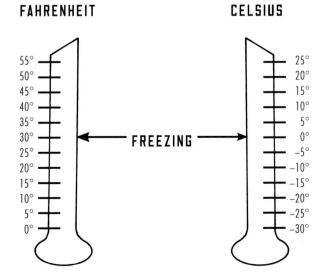

INDEX

MEET MATT MATTUS

Matt Mattus is an American plantsman, visual designer, and futurist. He is also a third-generation gardener of his family property in Massachusetts. Matt's popular gardening blog, Growing with Plants, has garnered recognition in leading lifestyle magazines worldwide and has earned a loyal following of fans. Matt is a trustee of the Tower Hill Botanic Garden in Boyston, Massachusetts, and is Vice President of the Worcester County Horticultural Society, the garden's governing board. As a noted plantsman he has traveled to many of the world's botanical hotspots from the borderlands of Tibet to the high Alps of Switzerland to photograph, film, collect seeds, and botanize the many rare plants in these native habitats. A two-term past president of the prestigious North American Rock Garden Society and an active officer in countless others, Matt is clearly a passionate plantsman. As such, he is a popular speaker at botanic gardens, specialist plant societies, and horticultural conferences. Matt lives in Worcester, Massachusetts, with his partner, Joseph Philip, three Irish Terriers, and countless poultry, canaries, and homing pigeons.